CONFESSIONS
OF A
BIRD WATCHER

Confessions
of a
Bird Watcher

ROGER BARTON

McGRAW-HILL BOOK COMPANY

New York   St. Louis   San Francisco
Düsseldorf   London   Mexico   Sydney   Toronto

1 2 3 4 5 6 7 8 9 B A B A 7 9 8 7 6 5 4

Library of Congress Cataloging in Publication Data

Barton, Roger, date
    Confessions of a bird watcher.

    1. Bird watching. I. Title.
QL677.5B368   598.2'073   73-16026
ISBN 0-07-003973-9

Grateful acknowledgment is made to the *Newark Sunday News*
for permission to use some of the material I had written originally
for its editorial page.

To Priscilla

Contents

FOREWORD

A man who is one of the most pessimistic and most successful of literary agents told me once that every book should have a beginning and an end, and that every book should hold forth a promise to the reader.

This book really began in Alabama when I was a boy and was first consciously interested in birds, and its end is my realization that environmental protection is the logical conclusion of an amateur bird watcher's activities, although an ecologist can still be a birder. I still hope to have tallied 600 North American species before my birding is done. The promise of the book is that any person can derive as much pleasure from birding as I have, especially if other members of the family cherish a similar interest. My wife and I have birded together since she was a girl.

A question frequently heard, especially from persons trying to make conversation, is "How did you first become interested in birds?" Strangely enough, this question is seldom asked among birders themselves. I was fascinated by birds long before I knew anyone else who held a similar interest. When I was in elementary school in Brooklyn, at P.S. 77, I used to go to Prospect Park before school to see what the birds were doing. None of my friends and associates was similarly inclined. My mother and father knew practically nothing about birds. I was never associated with bird clubs; the first time I was inside a bird club was thirty-five years after P.S. 77.

It is quite different for the young now. My wife, Priscilla, and I used to lead bird walks for the New Jersey Audubon Society, and members brought their children. Members of bird clubs now take their offspring to meetings and to lectures in the Audubon Wildlife Film series.

Persons are aided in becoming interested in birds by books, magazines, and binoculars. When I was a boy I had no bird books with colored illustrations; I had to rely upon the cards that were inserted as premiums in cigarette packages, showing birds in colorful if not faithful pictures. Later, some of the more affluent of us were able to buy Chester A. Reed's handy pocket guide for three dollars. These days our mail is filled with various bird and conservation magazines; I recall none in 1916 except *Bird-Lore,* published by the National Audubon Society. I was shortsighted as a boy, but owned no field glasses or binoculars. My only optical item was something I cannot quite describe, but it was a frame with two sets of lenses, and the smaller could be moved back and forth to put birds in focus.

My experience in writing a column called "Outdoors with Roger Barton" for the editorial page of the *Newark Sunday News* was instructive. During most of those twenty-five years the *News* had approximately 400,000 circulation. I found that my correspondence came in surprising degree from persons who were not birders, but who had been enticed to read the column and to develop an interest in birds; they ranged from garage mechanics to golf professionals, but most of them were middle-aged housewives whose major birding activity was to watch the creatures from their kitchen windows. So, I am happy to believe, I helped many of these readers to develop an interest in birds.

The 1960 Census of Population included classifications for bird watchers and hunters, and the number of bird watchers was some 11 million, compared with 12 million hunters.

There is little reason to tick off the merits of bird watching, because most of them are obvious. It is a clean hobby, and the reward for the participant is a clean reward, like seeing a scarlet tanager in a dogwood tree that glistens with white flowers. For some birders there is a competitive aspect, such as to see more species than his companions, or to break a record for the most species tallied in a single day, or to break his own daily or annual records, or to be the very first of his small group to find 600 species north of the Rio Grande.

It is a hobby that keeps one outdoors in fair weather and foul and gives him as much exercise as he wants. The exercise can be as great as climbing Mt. McKinley to see nesting long-tailed jaegers or as little as cruising along dikes in refuges, spotting birds from a motorcar. There are no exacting demands unless you care to meet them. If you play golf or tennis you must keep up with your companions, no matter how hot the day or how great your exhaustion. If you ski, you must go downhill no matter how troublesome your arthritis.

If you are a birder, you have little expense. Most of your trips are day trips and you take a sandwich, so the main cost is gasoline and highway tolls. A pair of binoculars will last you for many years; my German 10×50 war-service binoculars were bought at a pawn shop on Third Avenue in New York in 1946 for fifty dollars, and they are still superb.

I believe that a final consideration is the desire on the part of many persons to have a closer contact with nature, which left to itself is a relatively stable environment, compared with the relatively unstable heart of man.

CONFESSIONS
OF A
BIRD WATCHER

1

MT. SALEM FARM

I confess that I am an amateur bird watcher, in the sense that I do not make my living from ornithology. Until I retired a few years ago, I edited a magazine that helped advertising-agency media buyers and planners spend their clients' money most efficiently in space in publications and time on broadcast.

Yet, if your hobby is birds, as mine is, and if you pursue it over half a century, you find many species and become acquainted with even more bird watchers. In this time I have observed many more than 500 species of birds in North America north of Mexico, and have become acquainted with more than that number of birders, many of them through my weekly newspaper column. I do not recall the first bird I ever identified, but it was in Alabama in 1907, and either a bobwhite or a hummingbird, the question being that of precedence and not identification.

After spending close to forty years in New York in the advertising business, all between Thirty-eighth and Fifty-fourth streets, with luncheons almost every day at the Harvard Club, I decided to leave this business and retire to the country, where I could pass more of my time watching birds.

At that time we lived in Caldwell, New Jersey, which is approximately an hour's commuting from New York. We decided to retire to Hunterdon County, which is in the extreme western part of the state. The county has been described as "the last frontier between the Hudson and Delaware rivers." It is a pleasant rural agricultural area that is trying hard to protect itself against waves of people from city and suburban areas who increase school taxes.

It took more than a year to find a suitable spot. We wanted ample acreage, a brook, a view, a situation on an improved road, reasonable accessibility to New York, an open field, and both evergreen and deciduous woods. In those months of searching we drove more than 10,000 miles, the distance from Patagonia to the Arctic Circle. Finally we found the site we wanted, 25 acres in rural Pittstown, a dozen miles from the Delaware River. We called it Mt. Salem Farm, because historic Mt. Salem Methodist Church took a little chunk out of our frontage on the county road. We let a contract for our modified Cape Cod colonial house one March and moved in, on sleeping bags, just a year later.

One of the features of the house is sliding doors of plain glass that take up the whole sides of the study, kitchen, and our bedroom, so that we live with the surrounding pines. The house is built close to the ground, so we virtually live outdoors. In winter the low rays of the sun beam through the Thermopane with abundant heat; in summer the high sun streams in only in late afternoon. Our bird feeders are nearby, and we see the little creatures—chickadees, titmice, nuthatches, goldfinches—feeding when we ourselves are at table.

148 Farm Species

We were surprised by the abundance of birdlife at the farm. We have no water except our shady brook, yet have tallied 148 species in the seven years we have lived here. Apparently we are on a migratory route used by geese, hawks, and other species.

Priscilla and I are a bit diffident about lists, yet they add much to the intrinsic interest and competitive nature of birding. We keep four kinds of lists: our life list for all countries; that for North America; that for Mt. Salem Farm; and for the birds seen at the farm in one year. At the time of this writing, this last list is 104, which we consider poor, because, for some reasons we do not understand, we have missed species that were present in other years, as the barn swallow, purple martin, nighthawk, indigo bunting, and grasshopper sparrow. That is one reason why we were so happy about the invasion of northern finches in the winter, which added to our list redpoll, red crossbill, and boreal chickadee.

Scanning over our total list at Mt. Salem Farm, we find that the most predictable vocal owls are the great horned. We have yet to find some of the warblers such as the prothonotary and Kentucky, and it was six years before we discovered a yellow-breasted chat, right in the beauty bush beside our lawn. Our best sparrows have been the grasshopper and white-crowned sparrows, the best woodpeckers the redheaded, pileated, and red-bellied. Once we saw a snow goose overhead. We guess that our maximum count at the farm can be 168, including all possible species, and with our present tally at 148, every day can hold a surprise. Our last new species here was the rarest, a Lawrence's warbler. This is a hybrid between the blue-winged and golden-winged warblers.

Declining Bluebirds

A bluebird sang its soft gurgling notes from an oak near our house one day in late January. It is likely that this was a wintering bird rather than a migrant, although its song was long and held the enticement of spring. In our area the spring flight may arrive as early as February 22 in unusually mild seasons, but March 12 is a more normal date. The northward movement is surprisingly late, ending around April 10.

The number of wintering birds has declined in recent years. In the Christmas counts taken in December 1966, 11 clubs combing the northern part of the state from Raritan Bay to the New York line and from the Hudson to the Delaware discovered 46 bluebirds, all in three Christmas-count areas. In December 1970 only 23 bluebirds were found by 21 clubs covering the whole state.

A major factor which caused the decline of this attractive little thrush was severe winter kills in 1958 and 1960. The National Audubon Society in 1961 termed the bird a disaster species, and said that while it was in no imminent danger of extinction, it would take several years to recover. The extent of the decline and recovery is indicated in Christmas counts in Maryland and Virginia. In 1960, only 42 bluebirds were found in Maryland, compared with 778 in 1959. By the Christmas count in 1965, the number had climbed to 260. In Virginia, only 82 were tallied at Christmas in 1960, compared with 529 the year before. In 1965 the species had recovered to 244 birds.

In a document, "Rare or Endangered Fish and Wildlife of New Jersey," published in 1971 by the New Jersey State Museum, the bluebird was listed as rare, with a statement that the population had declined markedly during recent years because of unsuccessful competition with the starling and house sparrow for nesting sites. It added that placement of nest boxes in meadows and open areas is a worthwhile conservation measure.

Bluebird houses can be built or bought. I made mine from plywood, and the purchased ones are of a fabricated material. Inside floor dimensions are 5 by 5 inches, with 8 for depth of cavity. The entrance is 5½ inches above the floor and 1¾ inches in diameter. A smaller diameter may prevent starlings from entering, but it may also prevent the bluebird, heavy with egg, from getting in or out. The top is on hinges so the house can be cleaned of wasp nests and house-sparrow nests. There is ventilation under the eaves, and several small holes are drilled in the bottom for drainage. The roof overhangs front of the house by 2½ inches.

I place the house on a post (not a tree) from 4 to 6 feet above ground, in open sunlight. It faces away from prevailing winds that might blow in rain. Boxes are approximately 300 feet apart. A perch is unnecessary and tends to encourage sparrows. The box is of natural wood and may be stained but not painted. New boxes should be put up in late winter, as the birds are then on the wing. I leave mine up all year.

We have placed six boxes in our 5-acre field. Four have been occupied at different times by a single pair of bluebirds, but at the same time the others have been used by chickadees, tree swallows, and house wrens.

A day when we were picking wild strawberries in our field we looked into one of the bluebird boxes and found it held four nestlings. The same parents had a previous clutch of six eggs in a different box in the field, but these were taken by some human intruder. We had feared that, after this disappointment, the birds might desert our premises.

Bluebirds are persistent layers, however, and if a set of eggs is taken another will be laid in a short time. An old record from the days when egg-collecting was common and legal tells of a man who took five sets of eggs from one pair of bluebirds during one season in a Maine orchard. Another collector in South Carolina took three sets of eggs from one pair of birds, and allowed another set to hatch.

The two collectors were especially interested in these eggs because they were white, instead of the normal pale blue. Numerous sets of pure white eggs have been reported. A. C. Bent in his *Life Histories of North American Thrushes* tells of a study of 730 eggs of which 40 were white, a percent of 5.8. Birds that have been hatched from blue eggs have been known to lay white eggs, and birds hatched from white eggs to lay blue. There is no evidence that the laying of white eggs is an inherited trait.

Our last bluebird nesting in 1970 was successful, the parents feeding the four young on the periodical cicadas that were prevalent that year. Priscilla took excellent photographs from a blind set up only a few feet from the nesting box.

Friends of Bluebirds

An outstanding friend of bluebirds is Stiles Thomas of Allendale, moving spirit of the Fyke Nature Association. One year he placed many boxes in northwestern Bergen County, and reported 28 successful nestings out of the 42 boxes used by the birds.

Another friend is W. G. Duncan of Louisville, Kentucky. The bluebird is a passionate hobby with Mr. Duncan, and his influence is widespread. He wrote me once that he would be happy to supply bluebird nest boxes without charge in order to get the hobby started in New Jersey. When I mentioned it as casually as this in my newspaper column he received 704 letters of request. Needless to say, he no longer offers free houses.

Humble Oil & Refining Company has also done something for bluebirds. In 1963 it sent some 1¼ million bluebird houses to its customers. In a brochure accompanying the gift, the company noted that the number of bluebirds has declined, and one of the problems was housing.

Lost Homing Pigeon

One day a friendly pigeon landed on our lawn and remained for almost a week, probably attracted by the cracked corn and water we provided. The bird had a common coloration, but wore a band on its right leg.

Priscilla, who has a confiding way with birds, eventually coaxed it to feed from her hand. She read the aluminum leg band as AU 59 FALL RIVER 560. I telephoned the National Audubon Society headquarters in New York, which had a record of homing-pigeon numbers, and learned that the owner of the bird was Enrico Primo, of 379 Robeson Street, Fall River, Massachusetts. The Society added that Mr. Primo was a member of the American Racing Pigeon Union, Inc., and that the bird had been banded in 1959.

We wrote Mr. Primo, asking if he wished to have the bird returned, but received no answer. In a few days, however, the pigeon became more active, circling the house vigorously. Then it took off, apparently having recovered its strength. We wrote Mr. Primo again, telling him the bird had flown, and asking whether it had reached his house. Still no reply.

I have had many correspondents write about homing pigeons they have retrieved, but have found that the pigeon racing clubs did not wish to have their lost pigeons returned. This was because the cost of boxing and shipping the pigeon was approximately five times the original cost of the bird.

Why do homing pigeons become lost? One theory was advanced by Dr. Henry L. Yeagley of Pennsylvania State University. He maintained that the birds rely upon the spin of the earth and the earth's magnetic field to guide them. He tested the magnetic sense of pigeons by attaching small magnets to their wings. The birds became confused by the conflicting magnetic fields and strayed from their routes. Dr. Yeagley noted that this magnetic sense is confused when the birds fly near electric power stations or pass through radar beams. (See Jean Dorst, "The Migrations of Birds," 1962, p. 332, et seq.)

It may appear that our guest pigeon was a rather venerable bird, having been banded in 1959 and arriving here in 1966, but some pigeons live much longer. Average life-span of homing pigeons is eight years, but Kaiser, history's most famed bird, died at Ft. Monmouth, New Jersey, in October 1949 when he was more than thirty-two years old, having emerged from the egg in February 1917. Kaiser was a veteran of two wars and two armies. He was trained by Kaiser Wilhelm's troops, and captured by the Americans in the Meuse offensive in 1918. He died at an age which corresponds to 160 human years, and had outlived twelve mates. World War I produced many noted carrier pigeons. One was Mocker, twenty years old when he died in 1937.

Some birds stray away from their lofts and return after an absence longer than the life-span of most homing pigeons. One day in 1948 a pigeon belonging to a man in Cleveland returned from a 100-mile race it had begun in 1939. Appearing well-fed, the check-colored bird landed in the loft and promptly slipped inside to take its accustomed perch. In 1951 an Army pigeon that had been missing eight years turned up in a private garage in Tulsa.

Route of the Geese

Where do the wild geese go? One day in October nine flocks of Canada geese of a total of some 900 birds flew over our farm, heading directly southwest. The previous spring we saw Canada geese—with one snow goose—flying directly northeast. On one of these days I was in Hershey, Pennsylvania, more than 100 miles to the southwest of us, and the president of the bird club there told me that he and other members had noted thousands of the birds flying in a direction that would take them near our farm. We saw sizable flocks, perhaps the same, the following day.

What is puzzling is that important wintering grounds of the Canadas are along the Atlantic Coast, and a route southwest over Hunterdon County or over Hershey is not along the Atlantic flyway. I have seen immense concentrations of geese in the fall at Brigantine National Wildlife Refuge near Atlantic City, at Bombay Hook Refuge in Delaware and Blackwater Refuge at Cambridge, Maryland, on Chesapeake Bay, and at Lake Mattamuskeet in North Carolina. Some 60,000 birds congregated in the last place alone. All these places are reached most directly by following the Atlantic coastline. Why should the birds veer westward over our area unless they are headed toward some entirely different wintering ground, such as the Gulf Coast, and are seeking a different flyway, such as the Mississippi?

I discussed this subject with the American Museum of Natural History, the National Audubon Society, and Ducks Unlimited, but found no ready explanation. I consulted a dozen books and found nothing helpful on the birds' migratory routes. Nine hundred geese is a substantial number, and I am sure they were not of local origin. I went to Spruce Run and Round Valley reservoirs, the nearest sizable bodies of water to our northeast, but saw no geese.

Northern Visitors

The year 1969–70 was great for northern finches. Our first indication of this was in mid-November when we found a half dozen red crossbills in our pines and two boreal chickadees on our suet feeders. A few days later Raymond Blicharz telephoned from Trenton that he had seen 25 red crossbills in Washington Crossing State Park and an almost unprecedented 7 boreal chickadees, 6 in Hopewell and 1 in Pennington. He added that Richard Thorsell of the Stony Brook–Millstone Watershed Association had counted some 70 red crossbills.

Blicharz had other exciting news. In walking a mile or so around Washington Crossing State Park he had counted 35 red-breasted nuthatches and a saw-whet owl. He said that evening grosbeaks were abundant on the Princeton University campus. A friend in Stroudsburg, Pennsylvania, said that 50 evening grosbeaks had arrived at his place. Since our first sighting of red crossbills we saw them almost every day.

In mid-December, Blicharz reported that 217 red crossbills had been seen by him and others in ten places in New Jersey. Philip Del Vecchio of the Paterson Museum estimated that there were 406 red- and 396 white-winged crossbills and 34 boreal chickadees in our area.

Although the white-winged crossbill is normally a rare and irregular winter visitor, many of us remember the great flight in February 1953. Flocks of 50 or more were found in Caldwell, Verona, Montclair, Summit, and other places. One day my daughter passed a church in Caldwell near our house and found the ground under the hemlocks were crowded with these small birds. They were so weak and starved that they could be picked up by hand.

We were working in our pines one day in March when Priscilla suddenly exclaimed, "By gravy, that's a boreal chickadee!" The rather wheezy notes "aster-day-day-day" are quite different from the sprightly voice of our black-capped chickadee. We stepped near a suet feeder and saw the bird, distinctive in its generally brown appearance and dark brown cap. Our common species is grayer, with a black cap.

This was the first boreal chickadee we had seen at the farm since the previous November, when Priscilla discovered two that remained for a few days. At about the same time, reports from other observers indicated a remarkable flight of the birds, 10 having been counted in Hopewell on one day. John Bull in *Birds of the New York Area* writes that the flight of 1961–62 had previously been the most extensive, with a total of 22 individuals found in northern New Jersey in December. The first known record for New Jersey was a bird in Ramsey in 1913.

Our boreal acted more timidly than the black-capped chickadees. It visited the suet infrequently, and did not linger as did the others, but took a quick bite and darted away. It ate sunflower seeds in the same manner. We do not have the Carolina chickadee this far north; it is a more southern species that begins to appear in the Princeton area.

The boreal chickadee was known formerly as the brown-capped or Acadian chickadee. Its home is the spruce forests from northern New England to the limit of trees in Canada.

Vultures

Vultures have always impressed me, possibly because of my early acquaintance with them when I was a boy in North Carolina. When I went to the store through devious alleys, the big black birds were always there, performing their function as avian scavengers. One fall day, while driving near my present home toward Round Valley Reservoir, I saw 9 migrating turkey vultures in one group, 6 in another. Another fall day I saw 40 near Delaware Water Gap. The birds may go as far south as the Carolinas to pass the winter.

The adult turkey vulture has a red head, the black vulture a black one. The turkey vulture used to be uncommon or rare over much of the Northeast, but since the early 1900s has increased greatly in numbers. This increase is attributed to more numerous highways with the animal victims of automobiles they provide for scavengers; the increase in deer population and hunters, many of whom do not retrieve their kills, and the milder climates of later years. However, other typically Southern birds are pushing their ranges northward, as the cardinal, titmouse, mockingbird, and Carolina wren.

The black vulture is classified by John Bull as a very rare visitant to New Jersey, although it has been reported in most months of the year. Field identification is difficult. Although the black vulture has a black head, in its first year the turkey vulture has a leaden or nearly black head. However, the black vulture has a shorter, square tail, and a whitish patch on the under surface of each wing. Witmer Stone, in his *Bird Studies at Old Cape May,* says he always expected to find black vultures there, because his area is not far north of the bird's range, but, while he had studied hundreds of vultures, he had never seen a black.

Since the turkey vulture arrives in our area in mid-March, we were surprised to see one fly over our house one Lincoln's birthday. I do not believe this was a migrant, but rather one of the birds that winter in our region rather erratically.

In looking over Christmas counts of the previous year, I found only a single vulture recorded this far north, and that in Somerset County nearby, and only 2 birds at Brigantine National Wildlife Refuge, 50 miles to the south. However, in other years there have been found very unusual winter roosts and other concentrations. Around 15 were observed at the town dump in Hackensack all during the winter of 1954, and approximately 20 at a dump between Wilton and Weston in Connecticut. Throughout March 1958 some 100 were noted at Waterloo in Morris County.

Persistent Sapsucker

One day in April a yellow-bellied sapsucker alighted on one of our Austrian pines. It spent six full days on that one tree, in an area of the trunk not more than two feet long, and almost always on the same side. We saw it when we arose at 5:30 in the morning and it was there as long as we could discern it in the evening. It drank sap all day long, sometimes turning back its head as if swallowing in pleasure. Granger Davenport of Montclair says that at his place in Indian Lake, New York, one summer, the sapsuckers drank from the sugar-water feeders he supplied for hummingbirds. In another year a sapsucker ate berries on a Washington thorn tree outside my study.

A sapsucker can seriously damage trees by its borings. The injury results not from extraction of the sap, but from the accompanying destruction of the cambium layer which conducts the sap upward in the spring and downward in the fall. We were torn between protecting our tree and wonder at how long the bird would stay in one position. I have never read of any similar behavior by the bird. It was well we left the bird alone, because in subsequent years we saw the tree flourish as it had before the incident.

House Finches

House finches are still a little confusing to many birders. Since they are a relatively new species in our area, they were not mentioned in the guide most popular among bird watchers, Roger Tory Peterson's *A Field Guide to the Birds,* 1947 edition, the last. They are not included in Allan Cruickshank's *Birds around New York City,* 1942. However, the bird's status is discussed thoroughly in John Bull's *Birds of the New York Area* (1964), and it is included in *Birds of North America* (1966) by Chandler Robbins et al.

The house finch is mainly resident from southern British Columbia to southern Mexico, and east to western Nebraska and central Texas. This finch, or redheaded linnet, as it is called in many parts of the West, is the most common bird around dooryards. It is especially fond of nesting in vines around porches, in hedges, and in any place not far from a house. Once in the Mohave Desert in California, we found linnets nesting in a cholla cactus, a feat indicating the bird's adaptability.

The finches that are spreading widely over our state and the whole New York area are possibly the descendants of birds that were released from cages around 1940. A number of dealers in New York City had illegally in their possession caged house finches from California. When they were told the species was protected, the dealers released the birds, presumably on Long Island. First birds in a wild state were reported in Babylon in 1942, and subsequently in other Long Island communities, in Queens, Nassau, and Suffolk counties. The first report in New Jersey was at Ridgewood in 1949, but it was not until 1954 that they were reported elsewhere in the state.

Mrs. Howard G. McEntee of Ridgewood told me that her banding records indicated the majority of house finches did not remain in the same area very long, perhaps only a day or two. She wrote in 1966:

On any day with reasonably good weather the average number counted in my yard at any one time may be approximately 25. On a snowy day the number may increase to 50 or 60. On that same day perhaps 10 are trapped and banded, but at no time does the number of banded birds exceed 10 per cent of the total, so it could very well be that there had been 100 in the yard that day.

Since there are virtually no repeats in the traps, and the number of banded birds never exceeds 10 per cent of the total from December through April, it is a safe assumption that the daily turnover of the house finch population in any given area is tremendous. In each of the last two winters I have banded close to 300 house finches, and if these represent only a maximum of 10 per cent of the total, it is fair to assume that at least 3,000 visited my yard each winter.

That Mrs. McEntee's estimate of the large population is not exaggerated is indicated by the 1,388 house finches reported from New Jersey in the 1969 Christmas counts.

Care should be taken to distinguish the house finch from the purple finch. The house finch has a slender form, while that of the purple finch is more robust. The male house finch has a gray crown, red stripe over the eye, red breast and rump, and its belly and sides are streaked with dusky. The wing bars are white or whitish, and the back is dull gray-brown. The female has a uniform dusky appearance. It has no perceptible eyebrow line and no face pattern. Tails of the birds are square or slightly rounded.

The male purple finch is rosy on crown, breast, much of the back and rump. There are no streaks on the belly and sides, and the wing bars are pinkish. The female purple finch has a prominent eyebrow line, especially behind the eye, and has a heavy dark jaw stripe. It resembles a small female rose-breasted grosbeak.

We see house finches occasionally at Mt. Salem Farm, but rarely a purple finch. The winter of 1972–73 was exceptional, because we saw no house finches at the feeders, but 20 to 30 purple finches that remained all season.

Behavior of Starlings

One day the air around our house was filled with starlings, behaving in a most unusual manner. They were flying erratically, as if hawking for insects in the fashion of swallows. Another day we heard the screams of a red-shouldered hawk, and saw the bird wheeling in the sky and surrounded by some dozen starlings that followed the hawk in its every turn until it disappeared from sight. I have seen grackles and red-winged blackbirds harass a hawk, but never starlings.

Starlings are relatively new to our country, but seem to be assuming the habits of other birds. One is migration. Certain of the starlings are resident, but banding has shown that others are partly migratory. Being gregarious birds and apparently fond of associating with other species of like habits, starlings have joined grackles, red-winged blackbirds, and cowbirds in their wanderings in the fall and in their roosts, and have taken to following them south in migration. Since starlings fly faster than their companions, they start their migration later, but catch up with the others because of their greater speed. There are two migration routes in the Eastern United States, both northeastward in the spring and southwestward in the fall. One follows the Atlantic Coast states, while the other is west of the Alleghenies. The northeast-southwest direction closely parallels the flight of starlings in Continental Europe.

Unpredictable Waxwings

I frequently receive inquiries about cedar waxwings. The appearance of a flock of these birds in any locality arouses unusual interest. They like to come here in the fall to feed on the berries of the Washington thorn tree outside my study windows.

One reason waxwings create interest is that they are unlike most of the birds we know. They are seen occasionally in flocks or small bands throughout the year, but when they will appear or how numerously is quite unpredictable. They do not migrate north and south in the regular fashion of other species, although they are most abundant in our region in early fall. There is no close relationship between the times they arrive at their breeding areas and the times they nest. Although the first marked northward movement does not normally occur until May 10 in our area, egg dates have been recorded as late as September 15.

The waxwing is attractive because of its plumage and deportment. The feathers are soft brown and gray, with a broad yellow band at the tip of the tail and a touch of red in the wings. The bird's voice is soft and gentle, its manner is subdued, it is sociable and never quarrelsome, and it has the habit of sharing food with its companions. The waxwing has been called the perfect gentleman of the bird world.

The cedar waxwing's larger relative, the Bohemian waxwing, is extremely rare here. In 1962 Bohemian waxwings appeared at Princeton and Flemington Junction, but there were no other records for New Jersey. This waxwing is approximately an inch longer than the cedar waxwing, which it resembles closely. However, it has some white in the wing and chestnut-red on the under tail coverts instead of white. Both birds have crests and yellow bands on the tail. The cedar waxwing breeds in our area, but the Bohemian nests in Alaska and northwestern Canada. We saw numerous Bohemian waxwings one year near Anchorage, but missed them, not without a try, in New Jersey in 1962.

Aggressive Mockingbirds

A mockingbird comes to our feeders now and then, and appears to get along amicably with other birds. However, it does have the reputation of being aggressive. One of my readers says a mockingbird has taken a proprietary interest in a patch of *Rosa japonica* that is adjacent to a bird feeder. It chases away other birds that approach the area; it has cowed the cardinals and intimidated five blue jays in one tussle.

The mockingbird's aggressive personality is as natural as its lovely song. Its pugnacity is not limited to the nesting season nor to winter territorial defense. Encounters among the birds themselves are frequent, and as many as half a dozen birds will engage in bitter fights. They dive-bomb cats and dogs, and will put both to flight. They also attack their own images in automobile hubcaps and in basement windows. In spite of this aggressive characteristic, the mockingbird is so popular that it has been chosen the state bird in five states.

The mockingbird has been increasing markedly in New Jersey in the last score of years. In New Jersey in 1957 only 20 were listed on the Christmas bird counts; in 1958—29; in 1959—72; in 1960—95, but in 1969—1,219. Of course, over those years the number of counts increased somewhat and so did the number of counters.

Owls and Crows

One day we heard a great fuss among the crows, and suspected they had found an owl. Sneaking toward the center of the disturbance, we discovered a great horned owl sitting with dignified indifference high in an oak. The crows perched as near to the owl as they dared or flew around it, cawing loudly. Finally, the owl's patience was exhausted and it flew away, with a string of crows trailing behind it.

When an owl is discovered by a crow, the alarm is given, and all crows within hearing respond to the call. The owl seldom retaliates by striking one of its tormentors, but does get even when the crows are in roosts at night. Several crow roosts have been broken up by great horned owls living in the vicinity, and many owls have eaten crow. Blue jays rate a close second as enemies of the owl, but there are many more crows than jays around our farm.

The great horned owl was a bonus to our life at Mt. Salem Farm. We had long wished for a place where we could hear these owls, but did not know before we bought it that great horned owls would be our constant companions. There is a pair that lives nearby, and we distinguish the notes of the male and female, and Priscilla imitates them, even drawing them nearer. She has seen them copulating. There is a tall tulip tree nearby (we call it our goshawk tree, because there we once saw a goshawk perched) where the owls have perched in late day, pumping up and down as they sang their songs.

Other owls in our woods are the long-eared and screech owls. We find the pellets of the long-eared owls in our pine groves, and see one or two occasionally, but have never come upon a roost. Once we found the feathers of a long-eared owl in an adjoining field, and assumed (with the help of Dean Amadon of the American Museum of Natural History) that it must have been killed by a great horned owl. The screech owls are often heard but seldom seen.

When we walk through the pines we find many piles of feathers of birds—chiefly mourning doves, but also pheasants, two ruffed grouse, and a cardinal. We assume these creatures have fallen prey to the owls, as hawks seldom come down.

The rarest owl in New Jersey is the barred owl, according to the 1970 Christmas counts. Of the 152 owls observed, only 1 was a barred owl. There were 2 barn owls, 5 saw-whet owls, and 16 long-eared owls. Other species were short eared, 35; great horned, 40; and screech owls, 53.

Woodcock Dance

In early April we go at dusk to the lower end of our field to hear the flight song of the woodcock, a courtship performance.

These birds like the thickets along the brook, and fly over the lower ends of our own and a neighbor's field. We first hear the rasping *zeeip* that is uttered while the male bird is still strutting on the ground. Then, as it arises in ascending circles, we hear continuous musical twitterings, and finally the love song, a musical three-syllable note, sounding like *chicharee* uttered three times. The song is given by the bird zigzagging downward, finally landing near its starting point. We began looking one day at 6:30 P.M., and the performance was done in half an hour. It was still light enough for us to discern the dark forms of the birds against the sky.

2

WIDELY IN NEW JERSEY

Thoreau said he had traveled widely in Concord, and I have traveled widely in New Jersey. I have lived here since 1916, and have watched the birds all that time.

This has been a vastly rewarding pursuit, because the state is rich in birds and bird watchers. Some 400 species of birds have been recorded. This richness is favored by a varied terrain: 105 miles of frontage on the Atlantic with numerous barrier beaches; mountains that extend along the western side of the state and also cross it transversely, providing flyways for hawks and other species; freshwater marshes, of which the greatest is Troy Meadows; a sanctuary at Brigantine National Wildlife Refuge; some 2,000 square miles of wilderness in the Pine Barrens, an area of sand, scrub oak, and pitch pine.

People of the state have responded to this unusual situation. When I was president of New Jersey Audubon Society in 1954, there were 1,000 members; now the membership is 3,600. I have seen 1,000 persons at one session of the society in Cape May. The number of Christmas bird-count areas has increased to 22, and Cape May always ranks among the top 10 areas of the country for the highest bird count. Feed stores now buy birdseed not by the sack but by the carload. One survey showed that some 100,000 persons read my column about birds in the *Newark Sunday News.*

October at Cape May

Fall migration in New Jersey is most spectacular at Cape May, as the birds blown by northwest winds linger at this point of land before taking the long hop over Delaware Bay on their way farther south. If the winds are strong the creatures may be blown to sea, and I have seen them beating their way back to land in the morning, covering the sky like a vast umbrella.

Species we encountered in southern New Jersey over a long weekend in early October were impressive in variety and number. We tallied 140 species, but could not even estimate the numbers of flickers, tree swallows, hawks, and others. We stopped at Cape May, Egg Harbor Inlet, and Brigantine National Wildlife Refuge.

Memorable was the hawk flight on Sunday. The day was bright with a northwest wind, following a miserable Saturday with heavy rains. As we drove to Cape May Point we saw the sky filled with hawks, mainly broad winged and sharp shinned, but including red-shouldered and red-tailed varieties. The birds were not swirling in "kettles" that have been noted in Upper Montclair and Mt. Peter, New York, nearby points for watching hawk migrations. Rather, they literally jammed the sky, as if they had been blown to Cape May by the winds, and somewhat confused, were orienting themselves for their long flight across Delaware Bay and to southern wintering grounds. The day before, there was an outstanding migration of pigeon hawks, and on both days sparrow hawks were abundant, soaring overhead or perching on utility lines. The number of ospreys was noteworthy.

The autumnal migration of flickers at Cape May is one of the most striking ornithological sights of the region. We saw flickers on the ground, on trees, on houses, and flying overhead, an innumerable population. The movement takes place mainly at night, and most of the birds were seen early in the morning as they settled to feed and rest.

The air was charged with thousands of tree swallows in great driving, swirling clouds. The masses appeared like swarms of gnats. They lined the utility wires, covered roofs, reed grass, roadways. There were also impressive numbers of blue jays and brown thrashers. Almost every species seemed to be represented in unusual numbers. We saw a dozen yellow-bellied sapsuckers, for instance.

Near Lily Lake we discovered an evening grosbeak. Witmer Stone's *Bird Studies at Old Cape May* mentions no record so early as our October 2. However, the birds do appear in the New York City region early in October. There were also a dickcissel at the beach beyond the lighthouse, a red-breasted nuthatch at the entrance to Lily Lake, nine species of warblers, a loggerhead shrike, many cattle egrets, a red-bellied woodpecker, and a flock of bobolinks in fall plumage. Offshore, three species of scoters skimmed the waters, the common, white-winged, and surf scoters.

Brigantine National Wildlife Refuge, a sanctuary of some 19,233 acres northwest of Atlantic City, showed a different kind of birdlife. Noteworthy was an immature bald eagle. One redhead was the only duck of its species, and a white-crowned sparrow was of note. There were vast numbers of other ducks of many kinds, and the glossy ibises were numerous. We were fortunate to see both the sora and Virginia rails, as these birds are secretive, although their notes are often heard. We have seen clapper rails at the refuge often, but none on this visit.

Since there were few shore birds at Brigantine, we drove south to the beach along Great Egg Harbor Inlet, between Somers Point and Longport. The muddy shores there attracted piping and semipalmated plovers, ruddy turnstones, and black-bellied plovers, which we had found at neither Cape May nor Brigantine, while offshore the black skimmers plied the inlet.

Hawk Flights

The greatest day ever recorded for migrant hawks in our area was September 20, 1970, when 10,101 were counted over The Lookout on the Watchung Ridge in Montclair.

Members of the Montclair Bird Club and their friends manned the ridge from September 5 through October 12, and tallied a total of 13,398 birds of prey, 11,458 being broad-winged hawks. Outstanding among the ten other species were 5 bald eagles, 282 ospreys, 729 sparrow hawks, 687 sharp-shinned hawks, and a single peregrine falcon.

Fyke Nature Association of Allendale had its watchers view migrants from Mt. Peter, New York, just over the border between the two states, from August 30 through October 24, and the tally showed 5,186 birds of prey. Of note were a golden and four bald eagles. A golden eagle was seen also in 1968 and 1969. The count included 99 ospreys, 510 sparrow hawks, and 3,832 broad-winged hawks.

The migration was spectacular also in the western part of New Jersey. Floyd Wolfarth of Blairstown and friends watched from a high point in the Kittatinny Ridge near that community. One day they estimated some 3,000 broad-winged hawks and sighted a golden eagle and a goshawk. Also of interest were 20 ospreys, a pigeon hawk, 4 Cooper's hawks, and 12 marsh hawks. Priscilla and I also saw large kettles of broad-winged hawks swirling over Mt. Salem Farm.

Hawks in migration tend to coast along on the thermals or

updrafts from mountain ridges. They come from northern New York State and New England, drifting along the ridges to wintering grounds in Maryland and Virginia. As you stand on The Lookout peak in Montclair you can see the New England hawks passing over the Hudson River near George Washington Bridge and heading for Montclair. Thence they follow the Watchung Ridge across the state to the Kittatinnies.

Snow Geese

Great flocks of snow geese and a single peregrine falcon were the highlights of a trip in early November 1970 taken by the New Jersey Audubon Society to Brigantine National Wildlife Refuge. The number of snow geese was estimated at between 7,000 and 8,000, with 5 blue geese among them. Until recent years one never saw a snow goose at Brigantine, then a few appeared, and two or three years later it was a sensation when some 200 appeared. In a list of birds at Brigantine published in 1958, this goose was described as a rare winter visitant. In former years the only place in New Jersey where one could be certain of seeing snow geese was at Fortescue on Delaware Bay in spring.

The snow goose is white with black wing tips and is slightly smaller than the Canada goose. It breeds in the Arctic, and generally winters in the large coastal bays from Delaware to North Carolina. One spring day a snow goose appeared in a flock of Canada geese that flew over Mt. Salem Farm. On our last trip to Brigantine in the fall of 1971, Priscilla and I saw thousands of snow geese. Approximately 20,000 were there in 1973.

Birding in May

Bird watching in May is rather unpredicatble because of the vagaries of the weather. Normally there are four rather pronounced waves of migrants. A wave is caused when rain and cold dam the migratory current for a few days and then relent. Subsequent days of sun and higher temperature encourage the delayed birds to rush forward in great masses.

One May weekend Priscilla and I and a friend found 102 species in a field trip, although there was no wave. If there had been we could have tallied two dozen or more warblers, instead of only nine, and many common species that we missed.

Our first stop was Troy Meadows, called the finest freshwater marsh in the Northeast. It comprises some 3,000 acres around the confluence of the Passaic, Whippany, and Rockaway rivers. The most noteworthy contribution of the meadows was Virginia rails. I have found these birds rather secretive, but this day they were almost bold, strutting across the edges of little pools with no apparent fear of observers. Flycatchers had been unusual that spring, and the kingbird we saw in the cattail marshes was the first of the season. A quick look into Hatfield Swamp, which adjoins the meadows, produced a few more species, outstanding being a warbling vireo. This bird frequented a pond on the edge of the swamp, and we used to find it there year after year.

A good spot for warblers is a wooded ridge in nearby Boonton, and the outstanding warbler there was the golden-winged, with several in evidence. This is a conspicuous bird, with yellow wing patch, black throat, and a rather loud song that consists of one buzzy note followed by three in a lower pitch. We sighted two other flycatchers there, the phoebe and alder flycatcher, and an indigo bunting.

Next we drove 100 miles or so to Brigantine National Wildlife Refuge, which is on the edge of the ocean but contains large impoundments for the runoff of fresh water. There were several birds of interest, one being the cattle egret. Brant were numerous. There were several varieties of shore birds, including whimbrels, dowitchers, dunlins, black-bellied plovers, and turnstones. It was pleasant to see these birds in their bright spring plumages. Clapper rails were numerous along the canals, a bald eagle soared over headquarters, and a whip-poor-will sang at dusk.

As we drove from Longport, south of Atlantic City, through Sea Isle City to Stone Harbor and its rookery, we were impressed by the many brant feeding in the coastal waters. It was good to see that the heronry at Stone Harbor had not been affected by the winter's severe storms, for it was thronged with roosting and nesting egrets, herons, and glossy ibises.

Big Day

The Big Day is one—usually in the middle of May—on which particular groups of birders strive to find as many species as they can, competing with their own records of previous years. By now it is a venerable institution; the first one I recall in New Jersey was in 1927. Usually the area to be covered is scouted rather thoroughly before the Big Day, and birders may begin counting as early as 12:01 A.M., for the purpose of recording owls noted before the count.

Such a day was one enjoyed by the Trenton Naturalist Club on May 15, 1971. The club found 148 different species, a number that exceeded by five that tallied on the previous record count in 1967. The club's 50 observers explored an area around Trenton and Princeton, and in eastern Pennsylvania, especially the state park at Bowman's Hill.

The club found 30 species of warblers, including 3 prothonotary, 2 Cape May, and 7 Kentucky warblers. They found the worm-eating warbler at Bowman's Hill and a golden-winged warbler in the woods at Princeton.

A startling find was 5 evening grosbeaks feeding on weed seeds in Dutch Neck. Trenton Marshes provided king, sora, and Virginia rails and 6 least bitterns. The birders were fortunate in that their choice of a day was one that brought some new migrants, such as nighthawks and indigo buntings. Another conspicuous find was a dozen orchard orioles.

Operation Recovery

We have gone often to Island Beach to participate in and observe the bird-banding project conducted there each fall and called Operation Recovery. The project is under the sponsorship of the Fish and Wildlife Service, and its purpose is to record the volume, timing, and species involved in the fall migration along the coast. Island Beach is a barrier beach that is a state park, and it extends 10 miles along the shore, the Atlantic on one side and Barnegat Bay on the other. Banding stations situated from Maine to Maryland cooperate in this project.

One fall the banders of Island Beach tagged 18,573 birds of 132 species. They used Japanese mist nets, frail things that hold the birds but do not injure them, although some of the larger birds fly right through, leaving gaping holes. (The English use nylon nets of their own manufacture.) The record that fall offered some fascinating statistics. For instance, 1,359 brown creepers were banded. The birds came into the nets in twos and threes until September 26, when 155 astonished the banders. Even this number was exceeded on October 17 with 201. The extent of this phenomenon is suggested by John Bull's comment on the migration of the creeper (*Birds of the New York Area,* 1964): "Usually one to a dozen brown creepers are observed in a day during migration, but occasionally more are seen." The largest daily count in his records is 75 at Easthampton, Long Island, on October 5, 1946.

Species that exceeded the brown creeper in number were myrtle warbler, with 1,972 banded; junco, with 1,852; and white-throated sparrow, with 1,836. The only other species to top a thousand was catbird, with 1,263.

The rarest bird trapped was a black-backed three-toed woodpecker that appeared on September 29. Other noteworthy species and their numbers were saw-whet owl, 24; 1 olive-sided flycatcher; Philadelphia vireo, 35; a prothonotary warbler; a cerulean warbler; Connecticut warbler, 21; Kentucky warbler, 2;

mourning warbler, 6; a summer tanager; a blue grosbeak. The only northern finches were a handful of pine siskins.

Banders noted that many of the birds in this fall migration entered the nets from the south, indicating that the creatures had reached the end of the island, had seen nothing but water, and had decided to turn back. They were impressed by the large number of some species normally considered unusual by the field observer, like the Connecticut warbler.

Christmas Counts

Annual Christmas bird counts (taken in a period of two weeks or so around Christmas) were established in 1900 by Frank M. Chapman, who wanted to get persons' minds off hunting. He was then editor of *Bird-Lore*, the National Audubon Society's antecedent publication to *American Birds.* Only 25 reports were submitted and only 27 persons participated in that year's count. In 1971 a record-breaking 903 reports were published, and they enlisted a total of 16,657 observers. This was a year when use of tape recordings of bird calls and songs became an important means of finding species that otherwise might have been overlooked or missed, the recordings inducing secretive birds like rails and owls to reveal their presence.

In New Jersey there were 22 counts, each in a circular area of 15 miles diameter. Cape May, with 148 species, again led the state, lifting its cumulative list to 225 with the discovery of both black rail and glossy ibis. The Oceanville area, where Brigantine National Wildlife Refuge is situated, was second with 133 species, including in its list seven kinds of herons, glossy ibis, and 15 species of shorebirds.

Charles H. Rogers, curator of the zoological museum at Princeton, participated in this his seventieth Christmas bird count. He preceded me by some years as president of the New

Jersey Audubon Society. The first count in which I participated was in 1918.

Among the more unusual birds found in New Jersey on the 1971 count were both little and glaucous gulls at Barnegat; yellow-headed blackbird in the Hackensack-Ridgewood area; a king rail and two glaucous gulls at Lakehurst; black-headed gull and Bullock's oriole at Long Branch; golden eagle and Western tanager at Oceanville; house wren and Lincoln's sparrow at Princeton.

Year of the Cardinal

The year 1971 was the year of the cardinal. My readers reported an unusual number at their feeders, and at Mt. Salem Farm we had six pairs at our station, an unprecedented number in our experience.

The 1970–71 Christmas bird counts revealed a surprisingly large population of cardinals: Trenton Naturalist Club, 355; Walnut Valley, 320; Hackensack and Ridgewood, 288; Hunterdon County, 210; Sussex County, 196.

An analysis of the situation in the Hackensack-Ridgewood area was charted by Dr. Gordon M. Meade of Ridgewood, compiler of the Christmas counts for the two clubs. Fewer than 10 cardinals appear on their joint count in 1948, but this number jumped to 100 in 1953, to 200 in 1962, and to 288 in 1970.

Dr. Meade noted similar impressive rises for two other species that are relatively new to our area—house finch and mockingbird. House finches first appeared on the count in 1962, but only a handful. In five years the number was 145 and in 1970 it reached 255, almost equaling the population of cardinals. The mockingbird has had a less spectacular rise, not reaching more than 10 birds on any count from 1955 to 1964. Then the rate accelerated, and the total at Christmas in 1970 was 78.

Dr. Meade also charted the numbers of species that are declining markedly—bluebird and myrtle warbler. None of either species was seen in the 1970 Christmas count, compared with peaks of 36 bluebirds in 1953 and 125 myrtle warblers in the same year.

Dovekies

An exciting occurrence for birders is the appearance of dovekies on the New Jersey coast. Early in December 1966 an estimated 200 appeared between Shark River and Manasquan Inlet. One friend inspected jetties and counted 16 dovekies at Shark River Inlet, 5 at Manasquan Inlet, and a few each at Belmar, Spring Lake, and Sea Girt. Priscilla and I have seen the birds bobbing on the waves at Manasquan Inlet and have picked up dead dovekies on Long Beach Island. One day Betty Carnes, my predecessor as president of the New Jersey Audubon Society, had a dovekie brought her from considerably inland, near Carlstadt. Since these birds cannot take off from the land, she took it to Coney Island and launched it from a wave.

The dovekie is a small black-and-white bird less than seven inches long. It breeds in the far North, and ranges in winter as far south as the New England coast and sometimes farther south. In New Jersey it is a rare though regular visitant on the outer shores. Most of the records in our area come from Long Island. Ordinarily only a few are seen, and many of the largest counts have been of dead or oiled birds. A northeast gale is said to be the force that most often drives in the birds. Most are counted between mid-November and early March.

Breeding-Bird Census

A new kind of bird count is the breeding-bird census. It is more scientific than most counts, especially the Christmas count, in that areas inspected correspond to census tracts. It is sponsored by the Fish and Wildlife Service, which sets the areas to be studied on a random sampling basis. These censuses are taken in June, on the theory that any bird seen then is likely to be a breeding bird.

Two friends of mine took such a census one June day, driving 25 miles from Midvale to Newfoundland, noting the birds they saw or heard. They tallied 43 species, working from an hour before sunrise to 9:20 A.M. They stopped every half mile to observe for three minutes. The most numerous species was the bank swallow, one colony containing more than 100 birds.

Rare Bird Alert

Priscilla and I maintained for ten years or so a Rare Bird Alert. Its purpose was to let the birders of the state know when rare species appeared. We got this information from eight bird clubs. We asked each club that wished to participate to designate one of its members as an intermediary. He would let us know when a rarity appeared in his area, and we in turn would pass this information on to the other clubs. The intermediary in each club would notify his members when he received a report from us.

This alert functioned quite satisfactorily for a number of years, although it was expensive to us to maintain it. We spread reports on such rarities as green-tailed towhee, Say's phoebe, black-necked stilt, black-backed three-toed woodpecker, and a long list of others. We discontinued it in 1971 when the Linnaean Society of New York instituted a system whereby any person could call a designated telephone number and hear a recording of bird news in the New York area, including New Jersey. The news was furnished by Linnaean members and others, and the system was similar to the recorded information that had been disseminated by the Massachusetts Audubon Society for many years. This is now a joint venture of the National Audubon Society and the Linnaean Society, with the station at National Audubon.

Robin Fights Image

One day in April a correspondent in Dover heard a thumping against one of his windows. He found that a robin was flying against the window from a nearby evergreen. There was a string pull on the shade, and my friend assumed the bird was seeking the string for nesting material. He removed the pull, but the attacks continued.

Robins are noted for attacking their own images in bright surfaces, from windows to hubcaps of automobiles. Apparently they believe they are protecting their nesting territories against intruders. In our area, most of the egg dates are concentrated in late April. Like some other birds, robins establish definite nesting territories, determined no doubt by available food supply. Any male robin that invades another's territory is attacked vigorously.

One year a robin continued its assaults for sixteen days against its image in the window of a house in Kansas City, Missouri. Another bird fought its image in a garage window in Hamilton, Ontario, for five days. Douglaston, Long Island, had a window-pecking robin that returned in successive years to the same window. In Ponca City, Oklahoma, a robin pecked at its image in a hubcap for three days, remaining on the offensive for almost twelve hours a day.

If such antics are annoying, or if the bird appears to injure itself, the window can be coated with an opaque cleansing material that prevents any reflection on its surface.

European Goldfinch

One April day Mrs. Michael Dembicks trapped in Verona a European goldfinch that had been frequenting her feeding station. Several of us went to see it, including Frank Frazier of Montclair, past president of the Eastern Bird Banding Association.

Frazier banded the bird, although it had already been banded. He said that the old band number was of a series not used for wild birds in either the United States or Britain. The aluminum tag was a complete cylinder, indicating that it had been attached when the bird was so young that it could be slipped over the creature's foot. Frazier assumed that the band must have been applied by a commercial breeder. When adult native birds are tagged, an open band is used and it has to be closed with pliers. Subsequently he discovered that the bird had been banded by a breeder in Holland.

Bird watchers have long wondered whether the European goldfinch will once again become a breeding species in New Jersey. It was introduced at Hoboken in 1878, reached maximum abundance in the Englewood area around 1910, and spread as far west as Caldwell. I saw a mature male in 1918 in Rutherford, in the fields that then extended along the Passaic River. Soon thereafter the birds disappeared from New Jersey, but established themselves as a breeding species on Long Island, although the numbers there were not large. By the mid-1950s these birds had also faded out.

Search for Owls

Although we have seen long-eared owls at Mt. Salem Farm, we found none, only evidence of their presence, in a walk through our pine plantation one snowy day. Under a dense pine at the edge of a clearing, we found many owl pellets. These were blobs of disgorged indigestible fur and bones from an owl's prey, and they are a sure sign of an owl roost. Also in the area were traces of blood that must have come from a creature larger than a mouse; we assumed a cottontail. Otto Heck of nearby Rosemont, authority on owls in our region, stopped by for a visit, saw the pellets, and said they were undoubtedly those of a long-eared owl. Heck is so good at owls that on our 1970 Hunterdon County Bird Club Christmas count he found six species of owls between midnight and dawn: great horned owl, screech, long-eared, short-eared, barn, and saw-whet.

At two other widely separated places we found feathers of ruffed grouse. Both were from birds killed after the last snow. This was distressing, because we rarely see a grouse on our farm, so to lose two down the gullet of an owl or a hawk is a sad loss. We have seen and heard two great horned owls at the farm, and this fierce creature can dispatch a grouse with ease.

The red-tailed hawk has been known to capture grouse, and two of these hawks frequent our neighborhood. We saw one flying through the woods grasping prey which it dropped when we startled it. There were bits of mouse fur on the ground underneath.

Frequently we find little piles of mourning-dove feathers. The doves roost in our pines and are easy prey for owls. Occasionally we discover remains of a pheasant. Our most interesting find was the feathers of a long-eared owl; apparently it had been destroyed by a great horned owl, which is considerably larger and very ferocious.

Chukar

Once I saw a chukar partridge in Livingston, an escape from some game preserve, and recently I have noted that chukars have been listed in some of the Christmas bird counts. However, the manager of the state's Black River Shooting Grounds at Chester told me none had been released by the state. He added that the Nevada Department of Fish and Game had published an excellent booklet on the chukar, so I procured a copy. Called *The Chukar Partridge* (82 pages), by Glen C. Christensen, it is No. 4 in the Nevada Department's series of biological bulletins, and is published in Reno.

The chukar is approximately the size of a robin, with olive-brown back, creamy underparts with chestnut striping on the sides, and a cream-colored face with a black border. It is native to a vast land extending from Mongolia to Turkey. Beginning in 1931, chukars have been released in North America by game departments, gun clubs, and interested individuals in 42

states and 6 Canadian provinces. According to a poll taken in
1968, 6 of the states, all Western, had well-established populations and were hunting this game bird.

The chukar habitat in India, Pakistan, and Afghanistan, said
to be primary sources of birds introduced into North America, is
characterized geographically by a series of massive mountains,
including the Himalayas. The climate is arid to semiarid, and the
vegetation primarily grass with short brush. In North America the
major characteristic of the habitat occupied by the chukar seems
to duplicate the topographical and vegetational aspects of the
bird's native habitat. The male calls *chu-kar.*

Are Geese Changing Their Ranges?

Are geese changing their ranges? It seems so, with more
Canada geese breeding in our area and wintering farther north
than formerly, and snow geese occurring with much greater
frequency on our shores and inland.

For instance, a neighbor who has a farm pond, saw 2 Canada
geese rear a family of 5 on an island in the pond. The previous
spring around 130 Canadas alighted on the pond, and all save 2
took off the same day. These 2 remained for a few days and then
left, but our neighbor speculated that these lingering 2 were the
same who returned the following year to rear their family.
Incidentally, our neighbor says the geese cackle and warn her of
marauding dogs. This reminds one of the classic story of how
Rome was saved from sacking Goths by the cackling of geese
awakened in the middle of the night. Canada geese breed
throughout our area, and who actually knows, as is alleged, that
"the numerous flocks seen on inland ponds are for the most part
descendants of captive birds"?

Reports from Washington in 1970 said that modern agriculture and the creation of waterfowl sanctuaries have changed the
centuries-old habits of geese. That winter a half million Canada
geese, two-thirds of the Atlantic flyway population, remained on

the Delmarva Peninsula. Farther south, aerial surveys disclosed only 23,000 at Lake Mattamuskeet in North Carolina, whereas one year in the early 1960s when Priscilla and I were at Mattamuskeet, the number of geese was some 120,000. The Mississippi flyway has also witnessed this change. Canada geese once wintered by the thousands in the coastal marshes of Louisiana. The birds are considered rare in that region today. The story is the same for other parts of the country. Sanctuaries attract the birds, and corn and other high-energy foods enable them to survive hard winters.

Feeding Station

My friends Edward and Victor Wisner of Elberon, on the Jersey shore, are especially fortunate in the birds they have attracted to their feeding station. One winter they wrote that they were feeding approximately 500 birds, including some 200 each of mourning doves and house finches, 20 cardinals, and numerous evening grosbeaks, pine siskins, white-throated sparrows, and other species.

The Wisners were also feeding at another spot, windswept by the ocean, a mixed flock of some 200 horned larks, snow buntings, Lapland longspurs, and mourning doves. The count of 75 snow buntings in this flock was considered exceptional.

Sandhill Crane

A most improbable thing occurred in April 1970. A sandhill crane appeared in Yellow Frame in the identical field where the same or another crane had lingered the year before from early June through summer. It would be even more improbable if it were a different bird, although what would bring the same creature back to the identical spot is hard to imagine.

This is a busy place, within plain view of Route 94, and the field is just behind a farmhouse with a dog. The only other sandhill cranes I have seen were in the remote muskeg bogs of northern Michigan and in the Florida Everglades.

Although this crane used to appear in New Jersey, that was more than a hundred years ago. Recently there have been three or four reports of the birds passing through, but none of a crane taking up summer residence in our state and returning to the same spot another year.

It is a lordly bird, 44 inches long with a wingspread of 80. It is gray with red on the head. In the air it looks like a flying cross, and it utters a rolling croak that sounds like *gur-roo.*

Hazards to Birds

In late September 1970, birds crashed into the Empire State Building and were victims of a familiar hazard of migration that includes tall buildings, lighthouses, television or radio towers, and airport beacons. The Empire State, being one of the highest buildings in the world and on a flyway, has figured frequently as a deadly obstacle to migrants. I have picked up dead birds at the bottom of the lighthouse at Cape May.

I talked with the National Audubon Society in New York about that occurrence, and gathered that the flight must have been a large one, although the Society collected only 30 of the victims. However, these contained 20 species; most were warblers, including rare Connecticut and mourning warblers. The 6 ovenbirds were the most numerous of one kind in the small sample. There were also larger birds, such as scarlet tanager and rose-breasted grosbeak. This particular bird tragedy was attributed to a low cloud cover.

There have been similar occurrences in other years, particularly before the management of the building shut off the stationary all-night beacon during migrations. On September 1, 1948, there were recovered 212 individuals representing 30 species, including 10 Connecticut warblers and 78 ovenbirds. After a rainy night on September 23, 1953, representative species recovered were bay-breasted warbler, 63; Tennessee warbler, 42; magnolia warbler, 32. I passed the building on my way to work that morning and found dead birds scattered along the nearby streets.

Lighthouses with their powerful beacons have been lethal to birds. On the night of September 10, 1883, a great destruction took place at Fire Island. In a "bushel basketful of birds" that was picked up, the most numerous casualties were 230 blackpoll warblers. On the night of September 23, 1887, a total of 595 birds struck the light, 356 being blackpoll warblers. Fewer birds are reported killed at lighthouses than formerly, as beams revolve more slowly and apparently are not so alluring to birds.

Bird ladders, a form of latticework where birds may rest instead of fluttering disastrously against the glass of light, have been placed on some English lighthouses.

Alien Waterfowl

The tufted duck reappeared in January 1969 at Sam's Pond, Point Pleasant. This species had become somewhat familiar to many birders because in the winter of 1966–67, one of the birds appeared in the Hudson River opposite Edgewater, and was seen in approximately the same spot the previous winter. The duck obligingly swam across the river from time to time, so watchers from both sides had the chance to see it; Priscilla saw it from Edgewater.

The tufted duck breeds throughout most of northern Europe. It is a diving duck, and the male might be mistaken for a scaup except that it has a black back and drooping crest. A few of these ducks have appeared in the East in the past, but were supposed to be escaped cage birds.

The editor of *Audubon Field Notes* stated recently, however, that while the numerous sightings of Eurasian waterfowl in North

America are usually suspected of being birds that have escaped from private collections, a less skeptical attitude might be warranted. He says that if one looks at the breeding ranges of these species, it is obvious that only a slight mistake in direction could bring such strays to our continent.

European widgeons have become almost regular visitors to our area, and two were reported recently in the Delaware River near West Trenton. A teal, smallest European duck, appeared two years ago at Tinicum Refuge in Philadelphia. Another factor that might contribute to wanderings of the tufted duck is that its population has increased greatly in Europe in recent years, and its breeding range has extended.

3

ATLANTIC FLYWAY

Cape Ann and Cape Cod; Dalecarlia Reservoir in Washington; White Sulphur Springs and the Cheat Mountains; Nags Head to Ocracoke on the Outer Banks; from Jacksonville to Key West and other noted birding areas in Florida.

Cape Ann and Plum Island

A day in December spent watching birds off the granite promontories of Cape Ann and along the barrier beach of Plum Island was rewarding in the several rarities produced. It is a red-letter day for any bird watcher when he finds an arctic loon or gyrfalcon, but we were able to sight both, and in addition saw two snowy owls, a common eider, a black guillemot, and three noteworthy gulls, the Iceland, Kumlien's, and kittiwake.

The region is some 300 miles from Newark by motor car. Because of its more northern situation, it is visited first by arctic species; because of its exposure to the sea, it is the haven for oceanic birds blown in by northeast storms.

My wife and I were accompanied on this trip by her cousins, Mr. and Mrs. Charles Smith of Weston, Massachusetts, and by Miss Ruth Emery of Wollaston, Massachusetts, a member of the Massachusetts Audubon Society.

Birds at Halibut Point

Cape Ann juts 15 miles into the ocean off the northeast shore of Massachusetts. The nearest community to birding areas is Rockport. High on its northern edge is Halibut Point (some call it Haulabout Point), a jagged headland that has been quarried, but not enough to destroy it as a vantage point. We dressed in sheepskins and woolens, for the wind was sharp and the cold severe. At our feet flocks of purple sandpipers flew up and down, stopping to feed upon seaweed exposed on ledges by the low tide. The three species of scoters shuttled over the near ocean, and great cormorants, gannets, red-necked grebes, and red-throated loons joined the traffic in the air. Ducks were numerous, too, chiefly blacks, old-squaws, and common goldeneyes.

Andrews Point is near Halibut Point, but at sea level. The water there forms a kind of harbor that is favored by birds in stormy weather. A red-bellied woodpecker had frequented the point just before our arrival, but was not there on our day. However, almost the first bird that met our view was a common eider. This arctic duck had seldom ventured into Massachusetts waters in the two previous winters. Our bird was a female, rich brown and heavily barred.

While we were watching the eider a black guillemot flew in front of us and dived out of sight. This is another species from the north, more than a foot long, handsome in black and white. The guillemot is such a hardy diver that it sometimes remains in the Arctic throughout the year, feeding under the ice and coming up for a breath wherever it finds an air hole.

The guillemots and other Alcidae (razor-billed auks, thick-billed murres, dovekies) prefer Cape Ann because the offshore waters are very deep, hence suitable for these noted divers.

We also saw the Iceland gull at Andrews Point; it was standing on a nearby ledge with herring and great black-backed gulls. This is also an arctic species that in winter may straggle as far south as New Jersey. Two kittiwakes flew across our view; they are smaller than the other gulls, and while common on the oceans of the world, they seldom venture near the shore.

Rarities at Plum Island

Light fades quickly on winter afternoons, so stopping only to see a Kumlien's gull, a race of the Iceland gull, at nearby Bearskin Neck, we drove on to Newburyport. At this place in the extreme northeastern part of Massachusetts the Merrimack River broadens into Newburyport Harbor. Plum Island stretches from the harbor 10 miles south toward Cape Ann. There were numerous ducks in the harbor and many Bonaparte's gulls.

As we proceeded along the harbor toward Plum Island, we traversed familiar fields where a year before we had found upland plovers. Now the fields were full of hunters; we counted 15 in one area, all ready to shoot birds flying in or out of the adjacent Parker River National Wildlife Refuge. By the road was a house, and an immense snowy owl perched on top of the chimney. We learned that this house was occupied by the game warden, so the owl could not have chosen a safer or warmer perch. Sometimes the owls alight on haystacks in the fields.

Black Gyrfalcon

The northern part of Plum Island afforded hundreds of horned grebes and common loons, but it was the southern end of the island that provided the two rarities. Some distance down the island there is a compound where wild ducks feed, and we sighted flying slowly over the edge a great dark bird that was the black gyrfalcon. As the bird rested on a stump, we watched it through a 40-power telescope and could see its markings distinctly. The bird had been seen previously by Ludlow Griscom, and was found subsequently by a group from the Massachusetts Audubon Society. The gyrfalcon is another arctic bird, bigger than a peregrine falcon, but sometimes confused with the large and dark form of the latter's northern race.

Our last rarity was an arctic loon, formerly called the Pacific loon; it had been spotted some days before by the Massachusetts bird watchers, so we saw it, thanks to Ruth Emery. It was not far offshore on the ocean side, and similar in appearance to the red-throated loon. The arctic loon is a Western bird that occurs but rarely on the Atlantic Coast. John Bull admits only one sight record for New Jersey, but Griscom said that it had been found to be regular on the New England coast.

Albinistic Black Duck

I remember Plum Island for one of my more embarrassing experiences. With some friends I was driving down the island when to the right we saw huddled in the grass a dark bird with a white head. Having heard that snow geese had been seen on the island only recently, I assumed immediately that this was a blue goose and said so. When the bird was flushed it proved to be an albinistic black duck, all black with a white head. It was not a blue goose, but a black duck with a white head is also unusual.

Vacations at Cape Cod

We spent vacations at Cape Cod for several years between 1939 and 1965, generally at Wellfleet. There we rented a friend's old colonial farmhouse near Gull Pond. On returning one year, it was pleasant to find that a whip-poor-will still called nightly from the same clump of locust trees near our window where it had sung in other years. I had no way of knowing whether it was the same bird, but why should any other seek annually the identical spot for its nocturnal whistling?

I was near enough to the bird to hear the faint *chuck* that preceded the three whistled notes, but there seemed to be nothing about the call to distinguish it from the notes of any other whippoorwill. However, one observer who listened for an hour to a chorus of fully a dozen birds reported that some were distinctly better singers than others, that there were differences in tones and techniques.

Two land birds that made their presence best known by their calls were the bobwhite and the cuckoo. The former was amazingly common, whistling from the blueberry fields and salt meadows and from the dry hills where the pitch pine grew. One day a bird was perched in a tree by the road, and flew into the undergrowth as I walked by.

The black-billed cuckoos were common, too, frequenting the locust groves behind the house. Cuckoos were reported by other observers as rather scarce in New Jersey that year, and I had noted few. These birds are known for their liking for fuzzy caterpillars, whereas most birds prefer the smooth kinds.

In the years when we were there the Cape had been infested by hordes of caterpillars of the gypsy and brown-tailed moths. One year the area behind our house was practically defoliated; these two moths between them eat more than 500 species of plants, including conifers. Both species of larvae are hairy caterpillars that should appeal to cuckoos.

Whale Ahoy!

It is always an event to see a whale, and on the way to some birding we sighted one off Nauset Light. The light is at the head of the great barrier beach that stretches from Eastham to Chatham and is known as The Nauset. It is very similar to New Jersey's Island Beach.

My whale might have been 50 feet long, and was apparently eating its breakfast, idling in the ocean and spouting from time to time. One of the lighthouse men said they saw only one or two whales a year, although every year whales are reported from the Cape, usually off Provincetown. These seagoing mammals follow the migration of fishes along the shore.

Outermost House

A bit farther along the beach you come to the Coast Guard Station, and just below that, the fifth house down, is the place where Henry Beston lived a year and wrote *The Outermost House.* Beston built his house for a summer place, but decided to live a whole year in it, and to write about the birds and the tides and the creatures that live along the shore. The book was written in 1928, and the 1949 copy I possess is of the eleventh printing. Beston, a man from nearby Quincy, my wife's birthplace, experienced no hazards by living this lonely twelve months, for his house was only a quarter mile from the station and on a hard road. But he did have an appreciative eye for the natural scene, and did the sort of thing that Thoreau (who also wrote about these parts) could have done.

Cape Cod Mosquitoes

Cape Cod has its mosquitoes, but they are an effete breed. They do not pack the wallop of the Jersey mosquito. I have been bitten often enough, but these insects don't even raise a welt. You take a swipe at one and it practically falls dead of fright. Perhaps we Jerseyans are so thoroughly inoculated with mosquito venom that we are immune to the northern insects.

When I was a boy I lived in Rutherford, not far from the Hackensack Meadows, at a time when these wetlands along the Hackensack River were not drained and oiled and otherwise made mosquito-proof. I remember awakening of a morning and seeing the mosquitoes clustered on the inside of the screens, chilled by the morning air. I have spread a sheet of newspaper over a screen and killed 70 in a single operation. We who have survived this, what have we to fear from mosquitoes in other lands? When in Alaska, famed for the ferocity of its mosquitoes, I was bitten only twice one summer, and hardly knew it.

Soft-shelled Clams

You can have your cherrystones and little-necked clams; give me the long-necked clam that lives in the muds and gravels between the tides. Variously called soft-shelled, or steamer, or long-necked clam, it was one of the principal pleasures of the Cape in our early years there. A bowl of these clams, steamed, and a dish of melted butter in which to dip them, made a meal long to remember.

There was never any trouble in finding clams in the days before World War II when I visited the Cape, chiefly at Chatham, but after my return in 1947 they were scarce. Residents were a bit vague as to why, but the chief reason seemed to be that the clams just had not been able to withstand the appetites of the persons who wanted to eat them. Disappearance of the eelgrass along the shore was another reason given for the vanishing clam, as it was for other unfavorable phenomena for which there seemed no other apparent cause.

Horseshoe crabs and snails are said to be other enemies that retard the replenishment of the clam beds. The horseshoe crab, whose numerous empty shells shed in molting are found along the beaches, puts a squeeze on the clam to force open its tough shells. A carnivorous snail called the oyster drill is also the clam's foe.

Settling on a bivalve, the oyster drill quickly bores a neat, round hole through the clam's shell. Through this perforation, it sucks the soft clam, aided by a long proboscis that it inserts in the hole.

Earwigs

When we were in Wellfleet we read a dispatch from New Haven that told Cape Codders the European earwig had been sighted in several communities along Long Island Sound. Heavy colonies of the insect in Westport and Green's Farms were said to be the entry of the earwig into the metropolitan area. Cape residents did not know whether the pest would disturb them, but naturally were somewhat concerned.

The insect was not new to the Bay State, however, and periodically the South Shore of the bay is plagued by the pests. They are hard, brown creatures about an inch long. They have a pair of strong pincers or forceps at the tip of the abdomen. These pincers can give a strong nip.

Introduced into New England by a ship from Europe in 1911, the earwig is a pest indoors by its mere presence and the smell of creosote that it emits, while outdoors it feeds on tender plants. Earwigs may at times have found their way into human ears, but probably not with the intent to destroy the hearing of the sleeper, as it is popularly supposed. We found them at Wellfleet.

Shearwaters and Petrels

We went down to the beach at Wellfleet and set up our telescope on the sands, hoping to see some pelagic birds. We saw petrels and shearwaters; usually they live so far off land that they are seen only from ships. They nest in the Southern Hemisphere, and come north only in summer after the breeding season.

The sooty shearwater, which we sighted nearly two miles offshore, reminds one of a chimney swift. It is sooty, as is the swift, and has the same long, narrow wings and stubby tail. But there the resemblance ends, for the shearwater has a wingspread of approximately 40 inches and a length of 18. It glides over the waves on stiffly extended wings, tipping to one side as if trimming sail. The shearwater lives on squids and small fish, and, as does the petrel, it builds its nest in the underground chamber at the end of a 2-to-3-foot burrow in open ground.

The Wilson's petrel was much more numerous, whereas the shearwaters went by in twos and threes. The petrel is the bird that is sometimes called Mother Carey's chicken. It is also called sea swallow, which is an accurate name, for the bird is swallowlike in its flight and approximately the same size as a barn swallow. The petrels I saw had a square tail; the Leach's petrel has a forked tail, more like that of a swallow. Both birds are sooty brown, with white rumps. Both the Wilson's petrel and sooty shearwater are seen off the New Jersey coast, although the larger Cory's shearwater is the more common species; it is a bird that breeds in the Northern Hemisphere.

Dalecarlia Reservoir

For twenty-one years I was on active duty in the summer in the Army, and sometimes these situations provided interesting birding. One summer, for instance, I was with the Foreign Service Institute of the State Department in Washington, and spent the nights with old Army friends, Col. and Mrs. Brice Sumner. Colonel Sumner was in charge of the water supply for the District of Columbia, and his quarters were situated at Dalecarlia Reservoir, practically on the edge of the Potomac River. The grounds merged into a vast parklike area that ran down into the old Chesapeake and Ohio Canal, which in turn is only a stone's throw from the picturesque Potomac. As I lay abed at night I could hear the roar of the river in its deep, rocky gorge. The Potomac, which is the third largest stream on the Atlantic seaboard, supplies water for Washington.

The reservoir is in the wooded valley of Little Falls Creek, practically on the Maryland line, and covers 46 acres. Straight across the manicured lawns from the Sumner quarters was the filter plant. I have never seen so many purple martins in one place, swooping gracefully over the water's surface to capture insects, or lining up solidly on the power lines. I was interested to see how much gliding is done by this largest of our swallows. The barn and tree swallows beat their wings continuously, but the martin strikes a few beats and then sails along on the momentum of its flight. Most of the birds were females and young males.

In the parklike area to the rear of the quarters there were many fine trees, and some were largely covered with vines. In one of the trees there was a family of red-bellied woodpeckers, birds that are amazingly noisy, and trim in their zebra-striped backs and red crowns. This essentially southern bird is steadily extending its range northward, and is encountered much more frequently in New Jersey than the red-headed woodpecker.

I found surprising congregations of birds feeding on the fruit of black cherry and sassafras in this Dalecarlia area. Fruit of the cherry, which grew to considerable heights there, is said to be relished by 70 species of birds. In the trees behind our house I found bands of robins, of course, but the red-bellied woodpeckers were also partaking of the fruit. Blue jays came bounding in from time to time, and flickers, cardinals, mockingbirds, and mourning doves joined the numerous company.

There were several species that frequented the cherry trees but did not appear to be eating the fruit. Among them were the Carolina chickadees; this variety is smaller than our New Jersey black-capped chickadee, and I was able to distinguish its call as higher in pitch and more rapid in utterance. The tufted titmouse was also there and numerous red-eyed vireos. A yellow-throated vireo and two Canada warblers were in the treetops.

Sassafras trees grow tall in this region, and their blue fruit sitting on coral stems attracted birds. In one tree I found families of kingbirds and red-eyed vireos, the parents feeding their young. I notice that in New Jersey the kingbird has the same fondness for this fruit.

The Old Canal

The Chesapeake and Ohio Canal is one of the least-altered of the older American canals, and an excellent course for birding. It is no longer needed for transportation, although canal boats laden with coal, flour, grain, and lumber could be seen on its surface in the middle 1920s. It stretches 185 miles from Washington to Cumberland, Maryland, and its 12-foot-wide towpath makes an excellent way for bird finders. The canal is well filled with rather muddy water; it was approximately 80 feet wide in my neighborhood, but narrowed to 60 feet a short distance past the Maryland line.

I found blue-gray gnatcatchers along the canal. Pileated woodpeckers are seen in the dense woods that flank the canal over some of its course, and it is a favorite haunt of wood ducks. Overhead black vultures traced their broad spirals, and in migration it is excellent for warblers.

Amazing Mimic

How can anyone who is sensitive to birdsong sleep while a mockingbird sings all night outside his window? That was my experience one night in Dalecarlia. As I lay sleepless, listening to this amazing mimic, I tried to identify the songs of other birds that the mocker included in its repertoire. Some of them were easy to detect: the harsh cry of the jay, the crisp notes of the towhee, the *what-cheer* of the cardinal, and the *chirpity, chirpity, chirpity* of the Carolina wren. I was also able to pick out the notes of robin, crested flycatcher, flicker, titmouse, red-shouldered hawk, and, interestingly enough, the *teacher-teacher-teacher* of the ovenbird.

At this point I must have fallen asleep. If I had listened longer, I might have made a better score. Songs of some 23 species of birds and also a tree frog can be identified in a 90-minute tape recording of a mockingbird that lived one year on a farm in Weston, Massachusetts. I understand that ornithologists in the Washington area have heard the mocker imitate birds they have not seen in the area and, using this as a clue, have sought and found these species.

A generation ago the mocker was rare around Washington, but now is more numerous than any other species save the starling. At the Watergate Amphitheater on the Potomac, the birds participate regularly in the outside concerts, so that the mockingbird has been listed unofficially as the seventy-seventh member of the National Symphony Orchestra. Few heard the birds over the instrumentalists, but when the scores called for a rest, the mocker sang on frantically, in solo. When one guest star, a soprano, was singing, the bird flew to a flagpole over the stage and accompanied the soloist throughout her performance.

Fish Ladder

One day while at Dalecarlia we went to see the fish ladder that Colonel Sumner was building at nearby Little Falls on the Potomac. Purpose of the ladder was to help shad get over the 14-foot dam when they ascended the river to spawn. In the turbulent water at the bottom of the dam the engineers were digging what they called an attraction channel. It was a deep ditch, parallel with the dam, and created a strong flow of water into the fishway. The latter was a series of ten pools approximately a foot apart that enabled the fish to rise gradually and finally get over the dam. The design was worked out by the Corps of

Engineers with the Fish and Wildlife Service, and was said to be unique. The ladder would cost some $400,000, but it was estimated it might save $700,000 worth of shad each year. Colonel Sumner told me later that it did not.

White Sulphur Springs

For a dozen years or more we visited The Greenbrier in April, and it was an experience. This is one of the celebrated country hotels in America. The drive to and from Caldwell was just 1,000 miles. We generally proceeded down the Shenandoah Valley to Staunton in Virginia, and then southwest through picturesque Buffalo Gap and George Washington National Forest and over the Allegheny Mountains to White Sulphur Springs.

Although the higher reaches of the mountains were still bare, the roadways were brightened by redbud and dogwood in bloom, and on the hillsides were many flowers, conspicuously the trillium, columbine, and beds of phlox. The Greenbrier is 2,500 feet above sea level.

Some of the birds were remarkable. In one spot on the mountains we noticed a flurry beside the road, and stopping to investigate, found a flock of approximately a hundred chipping sparrows. Another phenomenon was hundreds of goldfinches high in the hardwoods on The Greenbrier grounds. Everyone remarked about the birds, so bright, so numerous, and so sweetly singing.

To see five orchard orioles and a prothonotary warbler in one tree at the same time is a memorable experience. Yet this was our happy lot on the grounds of the hotel at a spot close to the Greenbrier River. The orioles were two adult males, a male of the second year, and two females. The prothonotary was an adult male, with head, neck, and underparts rich yellow.

The male orchard oriole is handsome, garbed in rich chestnut and black. We heard its song, not so loud as that of the Baltimore oriole, but more elaborate and sweeter. In our area of New Jersey it is scarce and probably declining. We have seen it twice at Mt. Salem Farm.

The prothonotary warbler is rare in our region. I have seen it at Green Brook near Bound Brook and nesting at the Princeton Water Company Preserve. It is very partial to trees overhanging water.

By a spring we found five indigo buntings, three males and two females, and on a dry hillside saw a blue-gray gnatcatcher. The parula was always the first warbler we met when we entered the grounds, and it was so this time. Other warblers were scarce, the black-and-white and prairie being exceptions. We found 60 species in casual birding. Our big miss was Princess Grace of Monaco, who was staying at The Greenbrier, but taking her meals in her suite.

Swainson's Warbler

Once when Priscilla and I were at The Greenbrier, we found a Swainson's warbler near swampy underbrush just over the hill in front of the hotel. Dr. Lyle Bryce, the hotel naturalist, told us that the bird was not uncommon on the grounds, and that he found it most frequently in the very place we did. Later, this spot was used for construction, so I suppose the bird is gone.

We met there A. J. Russell, then president of *The New Yorker*, and an old acquaintance, who lived in New Canaan, Connecticut, and after his retirement moved to Hawaii. He told us an amusing story about his dog and a titmouse. The dog was a collie, and the titmouse was a frequent visitor to the Russell feeding station. One day Mr. Russell was working outdoors on some papers and his dog was beside him. The titmouse flew down to the table, and then darted at the collie, plucking some hairs from the startled dog's tail. The titmouse has traditionally used horse and cattle hair in its nest, but this one apparently considered dog hair an acceptable substitute. Some of our women friends say they have seen titmice gathering the combings from their hair. (Long-haired men, take note!)

North of Staunton, on Route 42, we stopped at a rural community called Mt. Solon to see a strange geological formation called Natural Chimneys. These are seven pillars of limestone that rise as high as 120 feet. They are topped by chert, and 6 feet from the ground show a horizontal band of lava that results from an old volcanic disturbance some 10 miles north of the site. There are tunnels that run through the bases of the pillars, and are believed to have been cut by an underground river, possibly the present North River, a branch of the Shenandoah. One of the towers leans 13½ feet, approximately the same inclination as the Tower of Pisa.

Cheat Mountains

Some years in returning north from White Sulphur Springs we stopped to bird in the Cheat Mountains. The Cheat ranges stretch for 30 miles, their elevation almost entirely above 4,000 feet, with Gaudineer Knob, where we did most of our birding, reaching up 4,445 feet. Between the ranges flows Shavers Fork of the Cheat River, a modest stream beloved by birds.

This is a great wilderness area, whose forests are not violated by a road or trail for 20 miles. There are stands of virgin spruce, and dense stretches of beech, birch, and maple.

Accommodations are scarce in this rugged region, but Mr. and Mrs. Dabney Kisner built a motel, primarily for hunters and fishermen, on Route 250 atop Shavers Mountain at the Randolph-Pocahontas county line. Once my wife and I had hoped to find a room there, but discovered all had been preempted by the Audubon Society of Washington, spending its annual Memorial Day weekend in the area. A tourist house in Durbin was our second choice. Other times we stopped with the Kisners.

Birds in the Mountains

At 4,500 feet birdlife is vastly different from that in the valleys. We found nesting juncos, red-breasted nuthatches, and winter wrens, for instance, birds that had long since left New Jersey for the north. We stood on top of the fire tower at the summit of Gaudineer Knob and looked down over the great spruce forest, hoping to see red- or white-winged crossbills. The crossbills feed on the waxy spruce blossoms, hence the best time to find them is mid-June, when the trees are in flower.

It was a memorable experience to stand on this tower overlooking the forest and hear the bird notes below, the magnolia warblers that nest in the spruce woods, and the hermit and Swainson's thrushes singing their evening songs. It was at Gaudineer Knob that my wife and I were searching the sky for ravens, and saw instead a majestic golden eagle soaring down the range. We also found a raven drinking from a brook.

Many warblers nest in the spruce and deciduous hardwood forests, and we saw the Canada, chestnut-sided, Blackburnian, black-throated green, and others. However, we missed the Cairn's black-throated blue warbler seen the previous year. This is a subspecies found in the area. Gaudineer's road is a likely place to see the wild turkey, and is the type locality for the Appalachian ruffed grouse. We did see one of these noble grouse strut across the road in front of us.

Mourning Warbler

The banks of Shavers Fork provided warblers, flycatchers, vireos, and swamp sparrows. Rarest was the mourning warbler, singing lustily in a rhododendron thicket. This bird is readily recognizable by its olive-green back, gray hood, and black throat. The warbler migrates chiefly west of the Appalachians.

The laurel was not yet in bloom atop the highest mountains, but brightened the lesser ridges with its white beauty. The most spectacular plant, however, was the flame azalea. This azalea grows 4 to 12 feet high, and is covered with big blossoms that are nearly flame color, or orange-yellow. Two other interesting plants were the northern Clinton's lily (*Clintonia borealis*), found on Gaudineer Knob, and the southern form (*Clintonia umbellata*), found around 3,000 feet. The plants are 8 or 9 inches tall, and the lilylike flowers of the northern variety are cream-colored, while those of the southern are white. Along the valley roads the lavender beard-tongue (*Penstemon hirsutus*) grew in abundance. The painted trillium was also attractive.

Along the trail we saw a large stand of lily-leaved or Fraser's sedge (*Carex fraseri*). Sedges are grasslike or rushlike herbs, but this sedge is quite unusual in that its leaves are an inch wide and 10 inches long, and it has a cluster of white flowers growing on a long stem that comes out of the basal leaves. It is characteristic of rich upland woods in eastern West Virginia. We now have growing at Mt. Salem Farm in New Jersey some of this sedge that Priscilla bought from a nursery in Ashford, North Carolina, and it appears to do all right, although it is beloved of cottontails.

Cranberry Bogs

Cranberry bogs, popularly known as glades in West Virginia, are noted for their remarkable plant and animal life. Although Cranberry Glades, some 50 miles north of White Sulphur Springs, are the most extensive, we visited a similar bog at Droop Mountain Battlefield State Park. These bogs have been called misplaced muskegs. They are spots where plant and animal life survived in the southern Appalachians after the melting of the Pleistocene ice, but where southern species also live. The bogs are composed of layers of sphagnum and sedge peat, up to 11 feet in thickness, which it is estimated took more than 9,000 years to form.

At least five species of birds reach their southernmost breeding limits at the glades. Numerous species of northern plants occur here in their southernmost known colonies. Birds that reach their southern limit are the hermit and Swainson's thrushes, the northern waterthrush, and the mourning warbler and purple finch; and some of the plants are the dwarf dogwood, goldthread, oak fern, and bog rosemary. This is the type locality of the West Virginia flying squirrel, and is noted for the golden-cheeked mouse. The most interesting birds we saw were blue-gray gnatcatchers.

En Route to the Outer Banks

Since I had been invited to talk before the Advertising Club of Norfolk, I believed this might provide an opportunity to drive farther south and become acquainted with the birds along the Outer Banks. These are the great barrier beaches that lie along the coast of North Carolina between the Atlantic and Pamlico Sound; they form a long, slender arm of sand whose elbow is Cape Hatteras.

On our route from home in Caldwell, New Jersey, we drove south 170 miles and stopped at Bombay Hook National Wildlife Refuge on Delaware Bay. Situated approximately eight miles east of Smyrna, Delaware, this refuge consists of some 14,000 acres of brackish marsh, relieved by various uplands that are wooded with hickory, tulip, oak, and maple. The name of the refuge is derived from an old Dutch name for the marsh, *Boompies Hoock.*

Bombay Hook

The first flock of Canada geese we saw included a magnificent snow goose that seemed dazzlingly white in the sun. The refuge is famed for the large population of snow geese which stop in migration; at times the entire Atlantic population of these geese has utilized the refuge marshes. That was a few years ago, before the snow geese began to stop at Brigantine National Wildlife Refuge in New Jersey, where as many as 20,000 may now be found in late fall.

The Canada geese have increased from a meager wintering population of 300 birds in 1950 to some 10,000 that were already arriving in considerable numbers when we were at Bombay Hook. When we were there in late October it was too early for the snow geese. However, it would make a worthwhile study to determine how the populations of Canada and snow geese have shifted among refuges on the Atlantic Coast since 1950.

We saw many species of ducks at this fascinating place, including shovelers and green-winged teal, also egrets and herons, Savannah sparrows and myrtle warblers, and innumerable cowbirds and red-winged blackbirds. A total of 275 different birds has been recorded at the refuge, including such rarities as the gyrfalcon, European lapwing, and pink-footed goose.

We took the ferry at Cape Charles (this was before the tunnel and bridge were built) and made the hour-and-a-half ride across the bay to Norfolk. Actually the boat left from Kiptopeke, and this area and the neighboring Fort Custis Military Reservation are on the very southernmost tip of the Delmarva Peninsula. Migrating land birds mass here in the fall very much as they do at Cape May in New Jersey. In the Christmas bird count in 1971, the tally of species at Cape Charles was 180 and that for Cape May was 146.

We had looked forward to the boat trip because we hoped it would show us some ocean birds, and we were not disappointed. Halfway across four dark swallowlike birds with white rumps passed the bow of the ship. These were Wilson's petrels, sea birds that often follow ships in loose flocks and are common off the Atlantic Coast in the summer, although this was late October.

Besides the countless laughing and herring gulls that followed the ship, we saw several gannets. These were both the

adult birds, which are white with black wingtips, and the immature birds, which are brown-black and take four years to develop
adult plumage. We saw the birds make spectacular diagonal dives
after fish. The gannets were passing along the coast to their
southern wintering grounds.

Nags Head

When eventually we crossed from the mainland of North
Carolina over a causeway that separates Currituck and Albemarle
sounds, we felt we were in another world. This was a land of great
sand dunes, and Jockey's Ridge at Nags Head is said to be the
tallest along the Atlantic Coast. This is the area where late
summer hurricanes muster fury for their passage north; Hurricane Helene blew sand through the third-story windows of the
hotel where we were staying. This is the spot where you take off
for trips to more southerly beaches.

Where did Nags Head get its name? Legend has it that in the
days of the pirates, the Bankers, as the natives of the sand banks
were called, lured pirate ships to destruction offshore. They tied a
lantern around the neck of an old and gentle horse, and led the nag
slowly up and down the sand dunes. Pirate ships at sea thought
this gentle bobbing light was from a ship riding at anchor in a
sheltered harbor, but when they tried to put into this harbor they
piled up on the treacherous shoals.

After leaving Nags Head, where we saw little besides golden
plovers, we drove south to Oregon Inlet. This is the first break in
the long barrier beach that is called the Outer Banks. The ferry
ride took half an hour and landed us at Pea Island National
Wildlife Refuge. Through the inlet the Atlantic pours into Pamlico Sound, making it one of the best spots for channel-bass
fishing along the banks and a good place for birds.

We saw the largest flocks of black skimmers we had ever
encountered. Three species of terns, chiefly the royal, thronged

the inlet, and dense numbers of laughing gulls followed the boat, nimbly snatching bits of bread thrown in the air.

Pea Island Refuge

Pea Island National Wildlife Refuge is a 5,880-acre tract just south of Oregon Inlet. It gets its name from the wild peas that grow there and which attract waterfowl. It is a grassy area, where freshwater marshes and lakes have been created by dikes. It was crowded with birds. I spent a whole roll of my film on a king rail that posed only 50 feet away across a narrow stream. We counted 33 whistling swans on one of the lakes, with 29 avocets, 80 snow geese, and 150 willets. There were innumerable Canada geese, widgeons, black ducks, and coots, with smaller numbers of shovelers, pintails, teal, and ruddy ducks. There were scores of gadwalls, and the refuge is said to contain the only large concentration of gadwalls along the Atlantic Coast. Boat-tailed grackles played around the edges of the marshes, egrets and Louisiana herons waded in the shallow water, and palm and myrtle warblers fed in the bayberry.

The refuge merges with the Cape Hatteras National Seashore Recreational area that extends down the banks to Ocracoke Inlet, 70 miles away.

Ocracoke

Until 1957 Ocracoke was accessible to only the venturesome, because it was separated from the upper part of the Banks by 59 miles of sand as well as by the two inlets. A paved road was put through in 1957. The former isolation left the countryside untouched and the herds of wild horses that roamed the island unmolested. One theory is that these horses are descended from animals abandoned on the island centuries ago by Spanish privateers. When the road was completed, the horses became hazards to motorcars and are now penned in ample acres. We saw them there, brown-and-white creatures, with golden manes and shaggy forelocks.

Ocracoke is fascinating historically. It was there in 1718 that the pirate Blackbeard was killed. The best-known shipwreck story is that of the "ghost ship" *Carroll A. Deering.* This five-masted schooner was found stranded on the shoals off Ocracoke Island in 1921, food still in the galley pots, but no crew aboard. The only living creature was the ship's cat. The fate of the crew remains unknown.

The ferry passages over Oregon and Hatteras inlets afforded views of many species of water birds. On the sand bars in Hatteras Inlet 47 miles farther south, there were hundreds of brown pelicans.

Lake Mattamuskeet

Going north again, and crossing Roanoke Island, we drove 50 miles through Virginia Dare Swamp to New Holland, one of the most unusual places we have visited. It is the site of the 50,000-acre Lake Mattamuskeet National Wildlife Refuge. This is lonely country, and the headquarters and lodge are well off the main road.

The lodge is a converted pumping station that was once used in an attempt to drain the 15-mile-long lake. It accommodates 50 persons, and may be recognized from afar by its 120-foot observation tower that was once a smokestack. Only two other persons were there when we arrived, a circuit court judge and his wife. He was really riding the circuit.

The lake was the haven for close to 50,000 Canada geese and 10,000 whistling swans. The swans had not arrived from the north, but the geese were there, including blue geese flying overhead, an unusual sighting. The most numerous duck was the pintail. We saw land birds, including the red-bellied woodpecker. Most abundant warbler in season is the prothonotary. Some 200 species of birds have been counted.

Reverse Migration

My wife drove back from Norfolk alone, as I had to make a talk that night, and at Cape Charles on the southern tip of the Delmarva Peninsula she found masses of migrating birds under conditions that reminded her of Cape May. After a strong northwest wind the night before, she found in the morning thousands of robins, ruby-crowned kinglets, Swainson's thrushes, and myrtle warblers flying in from the ocean and the south. The birds had apparently overshot the land in the wind and the dark.

Jacksonville to Key West

Two of the birds we wanted most to find in Florida were the red-cockaded woodpecker and the pinewoods sparrow. We saw both in the pinelands west of Jacksonville, with the aid of Samuel A. Grimes and Mr. and Mrs. Cecil Appleberry, Florida birders with national reputations.

Situated in northeastern Florida on the St. Johns River, just 21 miles from the ocean, Jacksonville (Jax, as it is colloquially known) has in its vicinity a wide variety of permanent and migratory species. For the woodpecker and sparrow we drove 30 miles west on Route 90 to the vicinity of MacClenny in Baker County. There we stopped at an extensive area of open pinewoods, the ground beneath the trees studded with scrub palmettos and covered with the short grasses and vines in which the pinewoods sparrow nests. Fortunately this was a chilly day in November, around 45 degrees, so the rattlesnakes had retreated to their burrows in the sand. In a warmer season, walking in these woods would be hazardous.

Red-Cockaded Woodpecker

With Sam Grimes and the Appleberrys we walked for two hours in these interesting flatwoods before we found the two species we sought. As we proceeded, we came upon warblers, as the pine, palm, and yellowthroat; robins and bluebirds, a white-eyed vireo, a blue-gray gnatcatcher, and red-bellied woodpeckers. An appealing denizen of the pinelands was the brown-headed nuthatch, an inch shorter than our white-breasted variety, with a brown cap instead of a black one. We saw both turkey and black vultures, and were told the latter is becoming scarce. This is because, being more sluggish creatures than turkey vultures, more are hit by motorcars as they feed on the highways.

We were first alerted to the red-cockaded woodpecker by its call, a rough, rasping *sripp.* Then, three birds appeared, moving actively from tree to tree. This species is approximately the size of a hairy woodpecker. It is a zebra-backed bird with a black cap and white cheeks. We saw its nests, generally holes on the south sides of long-leaf pines. Active nests are indicated by the resin which drips from the birds' borings around the nest holes. Some speculate that this sticky substance prevents insects from crawling into the holes. The nests are found only in so-called black-heart pines, those with cores soft with fungus. Such trees seem to languish; their limbs droop or grow horizontally, instead of at a slight upward angle. The red-cockaded woodpecker eats much the same insect food as the brown-headed nuthatches and pine warbler in whose company we found it.

The pinewoods sparrow is very secretive. We flushed two birds, but they disappeared in the undergrowth and we were not able to raise them again. It resembles the field sparrow, but is less rusty, and its larger bill is not pink. Most of the birds that breed in this area had left for wintering grounds farther south.

Fort George Island

One day, with the Appleberrys, we drove east from Jacksonville and came to Mayport on the Atlantic. From there we took the ferry across the mouth of St. Johns River to Fort George Island. The birdlife around Mayport and its marshes and beaches is similar to that of the New Jersey shore. We saw turnstones and plovers, herons and egrets, ducks and gulls.

Fort George Island was unique. A good part of it is administered by the Florida Board of Parks and Historic Memorials. It was one of the earliest sites in Florida to be occupied by the Spanish. In 1817, Zephaniah Kingsley, a slaver, came into possession of the island and developed a great plantation. He built houses and slave quarters which are still standing. We drove into the plantation along an avenue of live oaks and palms planted by the slaves. The damage done by Hurricane Dora in 1964 to the trees on the ocean side of the island was severe.

This area was very productive. Shorebirds fed on the flats, and sapsuckers, ground doves, Carolina wrens, and many other species were active in the fields and woodlands.

Friends in Florida

We have known Mrs. Appleberry for many years. She is a kind of institution among bird watchers. She and her husband lived in Jacksonville only five years before we saw them; previously they resided in Wilmington, North Carolina. There she won fame for organizing amateur birders so efficiently that one year their Christmas count of 169 was the highest for any area in the United States. Her place in Wilmington became a mecca for birders, and literally hundreds from many states traveled there to meet her and see her birds. She has been to birders along the Atlantic Coast what Mrs. Connie Hagar of Rockport has been to those birding along the Gulf Coast of Texas.

Key West

For Thanksgiving dinner Priscilla and I ate turtle steak and Key lime pie, and in the afternoon swam in the caressing waters of the Strait of Florida. Betimes we found a white-crowned pigeon in Key West Botanical Gardens on nearby Stock Island.

This pigeon is a West Indian species seen in the United States only at the southern tip of Florida and the Florida Keys. It is slate blue with a white crown. The population of the birds has been depleted by hunters in a state which allows an open season on mourning doves. We discovered only one bird, and it was wary. In Key West Cemetery we saw related species, the ground dove, not much larger than a sparrow, and the white-winged dove. It was surprising to find the latter, and Peterson (1960) classes it as accidental in Florida. We were familiar with it in the Southwest. However, John Watson, the ranger at Key Deer National Wildlife Refuge on Big Pine Key, told us the next day that the birds had been appearing in increasing numbers over the previous five years, and that 75 had been reported at Rest Beach in Key West. Robert Hermes, an Audubon Wildlife Film lecturer whom we visited in Homestead, said that a neighbor was importing these doves from South America, hoping to establish them as game birds.

Thirteen Herons and Egrets

This is a splendid area for herons and egrets, and we had a clean sweep of the 12 species described by Peterson, plus another which he does not list, the cattle egret. These included the great white heron, the largest American heron and the one with the most restricted range, and the Ward's great blue and Wurdemann's heron. The Ward's is larger and paler than the great blue heron, with greenish instead of black legs and a much whiter head. The Wurdemann's is a hybrid between the Ward's and the great white heron. It lacks the black plume of the great blue heron.

There was a lagoon behind our motel at Key West, and we noted that the great white herons and reddish egrets that fed there during the day were still foraging at midnight. Ranger Watson told us that on his night patrols he saw these and other herons also feeding at night. It was also interesting to note cattle egrets feeding at spots remote from cattle, as at the airfield at Miami International Airport.

Driving down the Keys

It is exciting to drive down the Keys. This is the winter home of the sparrow hawk. These birds and kingfishers were perched all along the electric lines. Palm warblers were literally swarming over the Keys. At Tavernier we saw four magnificent frigate birds, sometimes called man-o'-war birds, that were soaring overhead on wings that spread more than 7 feet. They are black, the males with orange throat patches and the females with white breasts. The tail is long and deeply forked, like that of the barn swallow. Frigate birds rob the gulls and terns, forcing them to drop or disgorge their food. In their flight they are said to be the most graceful and dashing of all birds.

Also at Tavernier two roseate spoonbills flew over the road, and at Bahia Honda Key, we photographed the Wurdemann's and enjoyed an excellent view of the yellow-crowned night heron. The beaches were crowded with laughing and herring gulls, cormorants, and royal terns.

Key Deer

When in Florida we stopped at Big Pine Key to see the famed Key deer. This diminutive creature is the rarest member of its family in the country. Its range is restricted to the Keys. Of several measured deer that have been killed along Route 1, which crosses Big Pine Key, the bucks have averaged 25 inches at the shoulder, 38 inches total length, and 33 pounds in weight—lighter than the typewriter upon which this is written. One that we saw was barely 2 feet at the shoulder. It was under the care of Ranger Watson of the Fish and Wildlife Service at Big Pine Key because it had broken its leg.

The entire population of these deer was estimated by Watson to be only 50 in 1950. Since then the Key Deer National Wildlife Refuge of some 6,750 acres was established, and the herd increased to 350. However, in that span of years, 270 of the creatures had been killed on the highways by automobiles. Hunters also shoot the deer from cars at night, cruising along the roads with spotlights. Such hunters, says Watson, are difficult to catch.

Loxahatchee Refuge

The Loxahatchee Refuge contains some 141,000 acres of Everglades habitat. This consists of prairie flats of low, grassy vegetation which are covered with shallow water in the rainy season of late summer and fall, making the Everglades a "river of grass." The rank sawgrass dominates the vegetation, but shallow lakes and sloughs abound in water lilies and water hyacinths, the latter exceptionally beautiful with their large flower heads, containing individual blossoms of blue, lavender, and yellow. The landscape is dotted with small bayheads—tree islands where redbay and Dahoon holly predominate.

Birdlife is scarce in late April. The lakes are too low to permit operation of airboats, so most observation of the refuge has to be done from the peripheral levees. We saw many cattle egrets on pasture lands adjacent to the refuge, but the other birds were routine. A total of 168 species has been counted there; the rare Everglades kite was once common, but is now seldom observed.

We saw a gray kingbird, typically a species of the West Indies that in Florida is commonest in the Keys. It has many local names, one of which, petchary, resembles its call. We have seen it also in Trinidad.

Flamingo

From Boca Raton, which had been our headquarters while at Loxahatchee Refuge, we drove down to Flamingo. Situated in the midst of Everglades National Park and on Florida Bay, this spot is farther south than any other in the continental United States, except, perhaps, Brownsville, Texas. It is tropical in its luxuriance of plant and animal life and is ideal for bird watching.

There was once a fishing village here, but in the early 1960s it was replaced by a new lodge, restaurant, ranger station, and marina. Around us were bays, lakes, and mangrove swamps. In one pool hardly the size of a football field, we saw 17 different kinds of birds. They included a great white heron, reddish egrets, 5 species of terns, some 300 dunlins, 37 marbled godwits, and assorted sandpipers, plovers and gulls.

The two birds that were relatively new to us were the great white heron and the swallow-tailed kite. The heron is a magnificent creature that is bigger and heavier than the great blue, and has a wingspread of nearly 7 feet. Most of the population of a thousand or so birds lives in the park. It is not especially hard to approach; one bird, familiarly named Pierre, came to the restaurant each night to be fed. The swallow-tailed kite is 2 feet long, with white head and underparts, black above. The tail is long and deeply forked. The birds float, soar, and circle with all the grace of a barn swallow. They prey upon snakes and rodents.

Thirty-eight miles to the east of Flamingo is the entrance to the park and the famed Anhinga Trail. This trail leads around a watery area and through original tropical growth. The air was loud with the grunting of alligators, and the monsters were seen sunning themselves on logs. Water moccasins coiled ominously on the lower branches of shrubs. The anhingas, or water turkeys, fished in waters teeming with gar, and perched with wings outspread to dry. We saw also purple and common gallinules among the lily pads and photographed them.

The limpkin was the bird in the Everglades National Park that impressed us most. This brown swamp wader is 18 inches long, approximately the size of the American bittern. However, it has much longer legs and neck, and a long, slightly drooping ibislike bill. We understood why it is called the crying bird when we saw it perched atop a tree uttering repeatedly its piercing *kree-ow, kra-ow,* as if it were in severe pain. You should never forget snakes when in Florida. The night before we reached Big Pine Key, two large rattlers were destroyed by Boy Scouts camping there. As I followed the boardwalk on Anhinga Trail, my eyes searching overhead for birds, I stepped over a 4-foot water moccasin sunning itself on the warm planks. Fortunately the moccasin is rather sluggish.

Spotted-breasted Oriole

I had to return to Miami to make a talk before an advertising group. Right across from our hotel, in a park on Biscayne Bay, we found the spotted-breasted oriole. This is a tropical species of striking brilliance and melodious whistling song that arrived in Dade County mysteriously from its home in the tropical lowlands of Central America. The bird was first reported in 1949, and now is on the official list of the American Ornithologists' Union. The oriole darted in front of us, a glorious display of flame-orange and black, and then rested in a low tree where we could observe it easily without binoculars. The orange-yellow crown distinguishes it readily from the Baltimore oriole.

Clewiston

This pleasant town at the edge of the Everglades and on the south shore of Lake Okeechobee produced two new birds for us, the smooth-billed ani and the painted bunting.

You have to look sharply to distinguish the ani from the boat-tailed grackle. However, the former has a weak flight and a large bill with a high curved ridge that gives it a parrotlike appearance. There seemed to be a dozen or so birds in town, and they constituted a colony that had existed there for several years. The anis are related to the cuckoos, and are not normally found farther north than the Florida Keys.

Another exciting find was the painted bunting. Two gaudy males and a plain green female were feeding on a heavily overgrown bank that bordered a sluggish canal. It is a thrill to see this bunting for the first time, as it has a blue head, green back, and red rump and underparts. No other American bird is so gaily colored. At the edge of the water near the buntings a 5-foot water moccasin lay in full view and glared at us defiantly.

All around the east, west, and south side of Lake Okeechobee is a great levee, 60 miles long and 18 feet above the lake level. We stood on top of the levee near Clewiston and watched the egrets and white ibises sail by, and a Caspian tern and many gulls, while other birds fed in the ruffled waters.

Nicodemus Slough

An exciting day was spent in Nicodemus Slough, a vast area of Everglades that is directly west of Lake Okeechobee and along Fisheating Creek. We left early in the morning from Clewiston with George Espenlaub in his swamp buggy. This is a vehicle that is a combination of jeep and station wagon, riding on airplane tires. George knows the Everglades intimately, and their birds, plants, and snakes, and by their scientific names. In the buggy we were able to traverse rough and swampy terrain and approach creatures more closely than if we had been afoot.

In one hammock, or little tree island, where palms and live oaks grew, we found a barred owl and almost stepped upon a pygmy rattlesnake. In another hammock we photographed young red-shouldered hawks. In the plains, where cattle were grazing, we found pairs of burrowing owls, and near an ancient Calusa Indian mound discovered a pair of nesting caracaras. We drove out into the grasslands and came upon five sandhill cranes, and here again were able to edge amazingly close for pictures. Everywhere there were flocks of herons, egrets, and ibises.

4

MIDDLE
FLYWAYS

Kirtland's warbler pinelands in Michigan; Chestnut-collared longspur prairies in Minnesota; Salt Plains in Oklahoma; Mississippi kite canyon in Texas Panhandle; Chachalacas to whooping cranes from Rio Grande to Arkansas.

Michigan Pinelands

Our objective on this trip was to see two birds, the Kirtland's warbler, second rarest of our warblers after the Bachman's, and the sandhill crane. I met Priscilla in Detroit, she having flown from Newark and I from Chicago, and after much delay because of stormy weather, we finally arrived at Pellston Airport. This is at the tip of the mitten to which Michigan's Lower Peninsula bears a resemblance, and is only 60 miles from some of the best Kirtland's warbler country.

The Kirtland's warbler represents the utmost in specialization. Its entire population is probably not more than a thousand. Its breeding place was unknown until 1903, when two fishermen found the warbler on the jack-pine plains of north-central Michigan. There it breeds only in an area 60 by 100 miles. The warblers first appear in a place nine to thirteen years after a fire, when the new pines are barely 5 feet high. When the trees become 18 feet tall, the warblers leave. This is because the bird nests on the ground, among a cover of blueberry, bearberry, sheep laurel, and sweet fern. When the trees grow high they shade out this ground cover, and the area is then no longer suitable for the birds. The trees are burned periodically to safeguard the habitat of Michigan's state bird.

Kirtland's Warbler

We first had our attention directed to the area by Olin Sewall Pettingill's *Bird Finding East of the Mississippi.* Before going to Michigan we asked Dr. Pettingill for the latest information on the location of the bird. We had known the Pettingills for some years, because we entertained them at our house in Caldwell when Priscilla was managing the Audubon Wildlife Series of lectures for Montclair and Caldwell and he was one of the lecturers. We also learned from the Michigan Conservation Department that the warbler might be found in the vicinities of Mio, St. Helen, and Houghton Lake, just in case the Pellston area failed us.

It was 106 degrees on the jack-pine plains, an area that resembles the New Jersey Pine Barrens. But we found the birds, at least five singing males. The Kirtland's resembles somewhat the prairie warbler. It is rather large, yellow below and grayish blue above. It has a varied song that possesses some qualities of that of the white-eyed vireo. It is exciting as a rarity, not as a bird.

Biological Station

We returned to Pellston to visit the University of Michigan Biological Station, where we were the guests of Dr. and Mrs.

Pettingill. Dr. Pettingill lectured there on ornithology. There were some 200 students, taking eight-week courses in zoology and botany. The station provides unusual opportunities for the study of birds, as it is situated on a 9,000-acre tract that lies between two lakes, and includes swamps, bogs, lowlands, uplands, and dunes. Approximately 150 species of birds may be seen there during the summer session.

While at the station Dr. Pettingill led us to a fascinating area called Reese's Bog. This is a mat of black spruce, tamarack, and white cedar on the shore of Burt Lake. As we walked through its shaded paths, we heard the tiny trumpet of the red-breasted nuthatch and the high-pitched, wiry notes of the Blackburnian warbler. Other warblers, thrushes, a solitary vireo, and a house wren sounded their calls or flew up in front of us.

The main glory of the bog was an orchid known as the showy lady's slipper (*Cypripedium reginae*). There were two stands of this magnificent flower, the plants two feet tall, the flowers fragrant, the pouch white and stained with light crimson-magenta. Dr. Asa Gray, father of botany in America, called this the most beautiful of all Cypripediums, and it is an accolade well earned. We found a stand of showy lady's slippers in New Jersey once, but the flowers had been eaten by deer. Wood lilies added their own grandeur to the bog, and there were lesser notes of beauty in the blue flags and twinflowers.

Sandhill Crane Country

We left the Pettingills to go to the Upper Peninsula in search of the sandhill crane, which breeds in the wild muskeg bogs not far from Lake Superior. The route took us north 90 miles, over the 5-mile bridge which crosses the Straits of Mackinac that join lakes Huron and Michigan, and along the spectacular drive that skirts the northern shore of the latter lake.

We made our base at Newberry. This is an old lumbering town that is 14 miles from the sandy road that takes one into the bogland where the cranes breed, but it is the nearest place where one can get bed and board. Now it grows celery. The local sport at Newberry is to take binoculars at dusk, which we did, go to the garbage dump outside the town, and watch the wild bears forage on its farther side.

We decided to make two trips into the crane country, one in the afternoon to study the terrain, and one the next morning when we hoped actually to see the birds. Normally you can drive from the improved road along a sandy trail to the first bog. However, several days of rain had made this impassable for an automobile, so we walked the 3 miles instead.

The country is wild and beautiful. It is sandy, but with many muskeg bogs. These bogs are on the sites of vanished lakes, are rimmed by tamaracks, white cedar, and black spruce, and in the higher sandy areas by beeches, sugar maples, and jack pines. The bogs themselves are covered with sedges, small shrubs, and various flowers. We saw the blue flags in bloom and pitcher plants holding aloft their strange reddish flowers.

There were no cranes in the afternoon, but we arose at four o'clock the next morning and were at the bog by five. On the way we met state police, who warned us to beware an escaped convict. We were skirting the edge of a vast and distant bog when we saw our first crane. It was standing in the sedge, made a few strides forward, and then took off, uttering a wild and defiant cry, a loud, deep *gar-oo-oo-oo*. We noted the bird's red forehead and its flight, neck extended and legs trailing like a flying cross. On the way back we saw five more cranes. They are great birds, with a wingspread of 80 inches, and they stand as high as a great blue heron. They are wary and wild, perhaps because they have been extirpated from most of their breeding range in the United States. Northern Michigan and Wisconsin are as far south as you can now find the breeding birds, although there is a related sandhill crane in Florida, which we have photographed. The similar little brown crane breeds in Canada.

On our way back we met two great horned owls. They were perched in a pine beside the path, and one flew off, but the other remained, allowing us to view it within a dozen yards. We saw no bears, although they often feed in the muskeg bogs, nor did we see the escaped convict.

Banded Purple Martin

On our way home we stopped again in Pellston and picked up a purple martin. This bird had been banded by the Pellston birders, who asked us to take it with us on our trip home and release it at an appropriate spot. Our first stop was in Detroit. The station was conducting research on the homing instinct of birds, especially martins. One bird had been taken to Wisconsin and released, finding its way back to Pellston in eighteen hours. Our martin was banded, and with dabs of red paint on the breast and yellow on the back for easy identification. We put it in a cigar box and took it on the plane to Detroit.

As I left the plane at Willow Run Airport, I opened the box, and out flew the martin. It rose above the buildings, circled twice to get its orientation, and then took off in a zigzag flight to the northeast. It should have flown northwest, but it is hard for a bird to orient itself immediately at an airport, where homing instincts may be confused by radar signals. The temperature was 91, the sky overcast, and the wind west at 12 knots. This was on a Monday, and we heard later that the bird had returned home by Thursday, in spite of difficult head winds.

Minnesota Prairies

Friends in Minneapolis, Malvin and Josephine Herz, invited us to visit them and see some of the birds in the prairies of northern Minnesota. We were happy to do this, because we had entertained them in New Jersey and they are excellent birders. Mrs. Herz is coauthor of *Where to Find Birds in Minnesota.* Mr. Herz, until he retired in 1972, was a magazine publisher. They are enthusiastic bird finders, and have been to the Antarctic and the Galapagos, to Africa four times, and around the world largely in pursuit of birds.

Minnesota has four times the area of New Jersey, so we had to cover 744 miles in Minnesota alone to find some of the birds we sought.We spent most of our time in Clay County, which is across the Red River of the North from Fargo, North Dakota. This was prairie, some of it dry, some moist, with occasional patches of elm, box elder, bur oak, aspen, and black cherry.

Chestnut-collared Longspur

Birdlife is similar to that of Eastern states, but with definite Western overtones. The species that impressed us most was the chestnut-collared longspur. There were scores of these beautiful birds in the dry grass prairie around the gravel pit near Felton. They breed in that area, and we were there early in June and saw them in their best plumage. The male has a black breast and belly, chestnut collar, white face, and a dark triangle on a white tail. We have seen the Lapland longspur in the East and the McCown's longspur on the plains of Colorado. The only other longspur is Smith's, found from Alaska to Hudson Bay.

The two-volume *The Birds of Minnesota* (University of Minnesota Press, 1936) by Dr. Thomas S. Roberts is recognized as one of the finest works in ornithology.

Clay-colored Sparrow

We have never seen the occasional clay-colored sparrow reported in the fall at Cape May in New Jersey, but Minnesota is the bird's home. It is a small, pale sparrow, with a light stripe through its crown and a brown ear patch. We identified it most readily by its insectlike song, five flat buzzes. It appeared in many spots, but chiefly in the brushy prairie northeast of Ulen.

The low prairie, sometimes marshy, is most attractive both in appearance and in the birds it provides. The floor of the prairie is dotted with blue, yellow, and white flowers, including violets, yellow star grass, blue-eyed grass, long-plumed avens (*Geum triflorum*) with its ruddy flowers, and puccoon (*Lithospermum canescens*), bearing heads of orange-yellow blossoms. A good find was the white lady's slipper (*Cypripedium candidum*), a small-flowered orchid that occurs from New Jersey west to Minnesota. The waxy white "slippers" are veined inside with purple. Several clumps were growing in one wet prairie. A friend who is a botanist said he had known of only one stand in New Jersey, and the last time he searched he couldn't find it.

The most spectacular bird species was the marbled godwit, a big tawny-brown bird with slightly up-turned bill, which breeds in this area of Minnesota. It is very noisy, insistent in its attention to us as intruders, and calling harshly *godwit* and *radica, radica.* In one moist prairie we counted a dozen, flying excitedly overhead. The godwit has made a comeback in recent years; as Roberts reported in 1919, "It is doubtful that more than an occasional pair remains to nest in some remote part of the state." This is the largest of our shorebirds except the long-billed curlew and the oystercatcher. We found godwits numerous in several areas.

Another rewarding bird was the upland plover, found on the higher levels around marshy places. Very attractive were the Wilson's phalaropes, not swimming and spinning in usual phalarope fashion, but running nervously along the margins of minor sloughs. In this species the female is more beautiful than the male, and in breeding plumage has broad face-and neck-stripes of black, blending into cinnamon. We missed the bird we wanted most to see—the yellow rail. We went to the marshy spot where it had been seen only recently, and, although the four of us approached the place from different directions, we saw no rail, nor did we hear it. It is said that the best way to discover the bird is to drag its area with a chain. Also it is desirable to get there while it is still dark. Two friends, Dr. and Mrs. Richard Chamberlain of Maplewood, followed us there in another year, and although they heard the bird's notes early in the morning, resembling the clicking together of two stones, they were unable to see the bird itself even though they were quite near where the sound originated.

Other Western Birds

We have seen dickcissels in New Jersey, but it is good to find them in their native land. The Western meadowlark, a distinct species, was everywhere. It is similar to the Eastern species in most respects except its song, which is loud and flutelike, compared with the slurred whistle of the Eastern species. Yellow-headed blackbirds sounded their rasping notes from the cattail marshes, but were not nearly so abundant as the red-winged blackbirds. We saw only a few Brewer's blackbirds, a Western type that is similar to our rusty. Impressive was the number of black terns that frequented almost all bodies of water; in New Jersey they occur mainly along the shore. Over one prairie we found two Swainson's hawks, a dark-breasted buteo that is more common in the Southwestern states.

Physical Features

This was our first visit to Minnesota, and we were impressed by the lakes; the number is estimated at more than 10,000. They were formed by glacial action which scoured out rock basins, dammed rivers, and left morainal hollows. It was interesting also to cross the Mississippi River at various points, notably at St. Cloud and Little Falls, where the falls have furnished water power. The soil is dark brown or black sandy loam of great fertility, suited to cereal crops. Most rewarding to us was to walk on what remains of the original prairie, which is rapidly disappearing into farmland.

Iowa to Texas Panhandle

We have done a fair amount of birding elsewhere along the middle flyways, even to Louisiana. One trip took us from Des Moines to Amarillo, Texas, 500 miles away in a southwesterly direction. We did not find this region very exciting, except that we would have liked to have spent more time in the Salt Plains National Wildlife Refuge in Oklahoma.

We started at Des Moines because I was giving a talk at the advertising club there, and ended at Amarillo, where I gave another talk and where, generously, they made me an honorary citizen. Bird watchers in Des Moines were helpful to Priscilla while I was busy with the advertising men. Woodward Brown, a member of the Des Moines Audubon Society, guided her to the best spots. Outstanding were the red-bellied and red-headed woodpeckers; it was good to see the latter relatively abundant, as it is disappearing from New Jersey. There were large numbers of migrating robins and monarch butterflies, since this was late September.

We found that we were too late to see the Bell's vireo, as it had left for its winter range in Mexico. We were too early for the Harris' sparrow, which spends the summer west of Hudson Bay, but winters from southern Nebraska and western Missouri well into Texas. It is larger than our fox sparrow, and in breeding plumage has a black crown, face, and bib. Later, we saw it for the first time, as a vagrant in New Jersey.

Birds in Nebraska

Next we stopped at Omaha to see our friends Col. and Mrs. G. B. Sumner, who were stationed with us at Picatinny Arsenal in World War II. Colonel Sumner, retired from the Army, was public works director of Omaha. Near Omaha is Fontenelle Forest, an area of 2,500 acres that borders the Missouri River. Its

virgin timber (oak, hickory, walnut, basswood, elm, and ash) is
the largest such stand within the state of Nebraska. Birds of
outstanding interest were red-headed woodpeckers and yellow-
billed cuckoos.

We drove south of Omaha some 20 miles to Plattsmouth,
where the Platte River flows into the Missouri. Here the state has
established the Platte River Refuge, an area of open plains and
woodland.

The first birds we noticed when we entered the refuge were
four Swainson's hawks circling overhead. This is a Western
species, proportioned like the red-tailed hawk and almost as
large. Its tail is gray above, not rufous as in the case of the
red-tailed hawk. This hawk often migrates in large flocks;
one year we saw a hundred or more on the arid plains of New
Mexico.

Various water birds have been attracted to two ponds in the
refuge. Of most interest was a white-fronted goose. It is a
gray-brown bird with a white patch on the front of its face and
with orange feet. There were also three snow geese and several
Canada geese. There were mallard ducks and blue-winged teal,
along with killdeer and greater yellowlegs. Resting quietly among
them was a Baird's sandpiper. This is a rather large variety,
buff-brown and with a back that has a scaly appearance. It
migrates along the plains, but appears occasionally in New
Jersey, as at Brigantine National Wildlife Refuge and the Hackensack Meadows. Low areas in the refuge were thronged with
red-winged blackbirds and cowbirds.

Through Kansas

After stopping in Kansas City, where I gave another talk
about advertising, we took the Kansas Turnpike and knew that
we would drive through the best area of the state for prairie

chickens. This is in the Flint Hills, a livestock-breeding area of bluestem grass pastures that lies between Emporia and Eldorado. I telephoned the biology department at Kansas State Teachers College, and was told that we could surely see the chickens if we could spend a few hours looking for them in a certain area, or that we might even see one flying across the turnpike. However, we could not spare the time, and saw none along the roadsides or flying, so missed this rare species.

At Wichita, where we remained with my brother and his wife, we found that the best birding areas were along the Arkansas River and the Little Arkansas River, which join within the city limits. Oak Park, which occupies a point of land formed by a bend in the Little Arkansas, has two ponds and rather dense woods. Sims Memorial Park, largely open prairie, is on the east bank of the Arkansas River. Here again, the birds were much the same as those in the East, although it was pleasant to see and hear the Western meadowlark again.

Salt Plains Refuge

Shortly after crossing the border between Kansas and Oklahoma, we reached Cherokee in north-central Oklahoma. This town is the entrance to the 32,000-acre Salt Plains National Wildlife Refuge. The refuge comprises 10,000 acres of salt flats, a 10,000-acre reservoir, and 12,000 acres of upland, forest, and rangeland. The major streams entering the reservoir are the Salt Fork (two branches) of the Arkansas River and Sand Creek. The salt plains are composed of minerals which remain after successive floodings and drainings.

As we entered the refuge we were delighted to find a small group of eared grebes on Sand Creek. This is distinctively a Western bird, almost exactly the same size as our pied-billed grebe. Individuals wander from time to time to the Jersey coast.

Its buffy facial tufts give it a look that is vaguely similar to a bird with ears. Another time we stepped through some underbrush on the edge of the reservoir and startled at least 200 white pelicans that took off in majestic flight to join an equal number of their kind at the other end of the reservoir. Some of these birds breed in the Northwest and migrate diagonally across the plains to pass the winter in Florida. I saw one in Cedar Rapids, Iowa, one fall, that had dropped down in this transcontinental flight to take refuge in a small lake, perhaps because it was sick. This was the first time the species had been seen in Cedar Rapids.

Our most exciting experience was to come across a flock of wild turkeys. A few of these noble birds are found in northwestern New Jersey. They have managed to make their way across the Delaware River from Pennsylvania, where they have been reestablished. We were eager to find the Harris' sparrow and asked one of the persons in headquarters if they were about. Outside, he said, there was a bush filled with them. We rushed outside and found they were house sparrows.

We would have liked to have spent days at Salt Plains Refuge. Its checklist of birds includes 251 species. Some 90,000 ducks and 30,000 geese find sanctuary there, among them 500 white-fronted geese. More than 3 million Franklin's gulls stop there during migration. We saw no persons at the refuge other than the rangers. This is one aspect of great Western refuges that appeals to an Easterner. Although Brigantine National Wildlife Refuge in New Jersey near Atlantic City is one of the richest for birds in the nation, it is crowded on weekends with bird watchers and with others who merely go there to ride around the dikes. Many of them do not even carry binoculars.

Mississippi Kite

Our last stop on this trip was the Texas Panhandle, especially Amarillo, where we saw some old Army friends and I gave another talk before a different advertising club. One of the main reasons for including this place on our trip was to see the Mississippi kite. This is a hawk of southern distribution, breeding only as far north as southern Missouri. It is a handsome creature, falcon-shaped, graceful and gray, with a wingspread of three feet. In the fall it migrates from the northern part of its range, so we missed it in the Great Salt Plains Refuge in northern Oklahoma. We did find it in the Texas Panhandle. Two of the birds were in a field beside the highway from Amarillo to Canyon City.

This was on the way to Palo Duro Canyon, some 20 miles south of Amarillo. It is surprising to come upon this canyon in the short-grass plains. It is a deep gorge through which flows Prairie Dog Town Creek. The canyon is a mile wide, with highly colored walls. A road takes you the length of the canyon, a distance of 6 miles.

Among the cottonwoods, mesquite, and juniper, we found several noteworthy birds. They included the golden-fronted and ladder-backed woodpeckers, black-crested titmouse, rock wren, Bewick's wren, Brewer's sparrow, and a cheerful band of bush-tits. These were distinctively Western species, in contrast to the birds we had seen in Iowa and eastern Nebraska, which were almost the same as our Eastern species. Yet the distance from Des Moines to Amarillo is only 500 miles.

Along the Rio Grande

If you want to find Mexican birds that breed nowhere else in the United States, go to the Brownsville-Harlingen area in Texas. This region is along the Rio Grande where it meets the Gulf of Mexico, and is farther south than any other part of our country. In late March it is rich in migratory birds as well as in semitropical resident species. Priscilla and I were birding there with Dr. and Mrs. Richard Chamberlain of Maplewood, who had come down from a medical convention in Dallas.

The two areas that are especially rewarding for the bird watcher are Laguna Atascosa and Santa Ana National Wildlife refuges. The former includes 42,000 acres of coastal prairies, salt flats, low ridges supporting thorny shrubs, and brushlands covered with mesquite, huisache (a small tree blooming then with yellowish-orange flowers), cacti, and yuccas. This refuge also embraces three lakes; one of them, Laguna Atascosa, covers 3,200 surface acres. Over the past ten years, 315 different species of birds had been observed at the refuge. We saw 99 of these the first day we explored it. We benefited greatly the first day from the guidance of Luther Goldman, then superintendent of the two refuges.

A dominant bird was the noisy and amusing boat-tailed grackle, which there was called the mesquite grackle. It was rivaled for attention by the scissor-tailed flycatcher, a bird that is strikingly handsome in pearl-gray, white, and pink, and which has a deeply forked tail that is two-thirds its 14-inch length. It chatters incessantly, and flies vertically in a zigzag fashion, rapidly opening and closing its tail. Another flycatcher was the vermilion, a small active bird whose underparts are flaming red. The Couch's kingbird is the common species of the Lower Rio Grande, and we found also the Say's phoebe that looks much like a small robin.

Most spectacular of the hawks was Audubon's caracara, a great black-and-white bird with a red face. My favorite, however, was Harris' hawk, a black buteo with a white rump and a white band at the tip of its tail. The Sennett's white-tailed hawk is a trim creature, largely white and gray, with rust-red shoulders.

The roads that wind around Laguna Atascosa and Cayo Atascosa (a bay six miles long) were sometimes underwater, but they afforded vantage points from which to observe a rich variety of shore and water birds. We saw four species of gulls, including the Franklin's, and five kinds of terns, including the gull-billed and royal terns. In one place we came upon a flock of two dozen white pelicans, and in another cove we were excited to find a roseate spoonbill, a score of white ibises, and reddish egrets, Louisiana herons, long-billed curlews, and other handsome species of wading birds. The birds were not startled by overhead planes, but the helicopters frightened them, as the machines must have looked like hovering hawks.

It is impossible to suggest adequately here the marvelous variety of birdlife at this refuge and the strikingly beautiful and interesting surroundings in which the birds were living. I haven't mentioned the mottled ducks or the Cassin's sparrows, or others of the 21 species which I saw for the first time.

Santa Ana Refuge

Harlingen is not far from Brownsville, and if you drive 40 miles southwest from Harlingen you come to a lowland flanking a big bend of the Rio Grande. Two thousand acres of this are included in the Santa Ana Wildlife Refuge, which was established by the U.S. Fish and Wildlife Service in 1943. It is an area made green by a junglelike forest of hackberry, elm, ebony, ash, anacua, and tepehuaje trees that have a dense understory of vines and shrubs. Many of the trees are festooned with Spanish moss. Besides the water boundary of the river, there are two small inland ponds that are beloved of waterfowl and wading birds. Over the previous decade, 249 species of birds have been observed on the reservation, and for us it produced some of the most attractive and characteristic birds of the Lower Rio Grande. First were the chachalacas. These creatures are at their noisy best early in the morning, and almost immediately when we drove into the refuge we heard them uttering the loud three-syllable notes *cha'-ca-lac,* from which they get their name. They are like small turkeys, almost 2 feet long, and brown with greenish tails. They perch in treetops and hide in dense thickets. Chachalacas are rapidly disappearing from along the Rio Grande as farmers destroy the underbrush.

Three equally noisy birds, but all more colorful, were the green jay; the kiskadee, or derby flycatcher; and the golden-fronted woodpecker. The first was our favorite bird of the trip, a nervous, pugnacious, bright species that has a dark-green back, light-green underparts, blue head, black throat, and big yellow outer tail feathers. It is almost a foot long. The kiskadee flycatcher is a heavy bird, and almost as long as the jay. It acts like a kingfisher, perching over water and diving after small fish. Its head and face are streaked with black, white, and yellow, and its underparts are bright sulphur. It was to be several years before we became reacquainted with this bird in Trinidad. The golden-fronted woodpecker is somewhat shorter than the flicker, but with the same white rump patch. It has a zebra-striped back, and yellow, red, and orange, respectively, on forehead, crown, and nape.

Least Grebe

On one of the ponds we found the least grebe, sometimes called the Mexican grebe. This species is only 9 inches long; it was with coots and a common gallinule. Around headquarters the brilliant hooded orioles called from high in the trees, and white-fronted doves made their hollow cooing notes while feeding on the ground. We saw also the Inca, ground, and mourning doves.

I make only casual mention of the upland plovers that we found so plentiful on the airfields at Houston and Corpus Christi, or the sage thrasher whose identification we debated so long, or the great horned owl that hardly moved all day from its favorite tree. The roadrunners also gave us many fine views, and we saw them sing their cuckoolike songs, produced laboriously as if each note had been stuck in the bird's throat.

Port Isabel

Port Isabel and the surrounding country were also rewarding. The port is near the southern end of a 120-mile-long barrier beach called Padre Island that separates Laguna Madre from the Gulf of Mexico. On the beaches we saw marbled godwits, whimbrels, and numerous other species. We got good pictures of willets.

Nothing has been said of the flowers we saw on this trip. The tall prickly poppy displayed its yellow and white blooms, and fields were carpeted with sand verbena and an evening primrose called amapolito. We were too early for the flowering of the opuntia cactus, but another time we'll see its yellow flowers and hit the warbler wave which had hardly begun. Maybe, also, we will find some of the birds we missed, the varied and painted buntings, the jacana, and the little green kingfisher.

Snakebite

Our friends the Chamberlains left us in Brownsville, whence we flew to New York, and they drove to visit the famous King Ranch, which is one of the largest cattle ranches in the world, larger than the entire state of Rhode Island. Tommy, as Mrs. Chamberlain is called, drove off toward the end of their stay there to photograph some desert flowers that she thought might interest Priscilla. Just as she snapped a picture of an attractive stand, she felt a blow at her ankle and leaned over to see what had hit her. To her horror she saw a 5-foot diamondback rattlesnake recoiling after having sunk its fangs in her ankle. She had studied skins in the museum in Dallas. The fang marks were an inch apart and were oozing blood. She broke all speed marks back to her motel, and from there Dr. Chamberlain took her to the hospital in Kingsville. She was given intravenous injections of cortisone, and incisions were made around the punctures and suction cups applied to pull out the poison. She was able to leave the hospital after a few hours. One explanation for her speedy release was that the snake had apparently fed on a rabbit just before it bit Tommy, so its poison had been largely expended.

Whooping Cranes

My wife and I had the most memorable experience in our years of birding when we photographed two whooping cranes from within 50 feet. This was four years after our first visit to the Rio Grande.

We had taken Willie Close's cabin cruiser out of Rockport, Texas, had made our way up the Gulf Intracoastal Waterway through Aransas Bay to Blackjack Peninsula. The peninsula is the southern end of the Aransas National Wildlife Refuge, the winter home of the world's last flock of whooping cranes. We came upon the birds just as we reached the tip of the peninsula. The water is quite shallow beside the channel, and the pair of magnificent white birds fed unafraid while I clicked off a whole roll of 35-mm film.

As we proceeded 35 miles up the waterway to a point nearly opposite the observation tower in the refuge where persons ordinarily watch for the birds, we passed 9 other cranes. There were 38 at the refuge that year. These great creatures have a wingspread of 7½ feet and stand 5 feet high. They are the most spectacular and celebrated of American birds. Next to the ivory-billed woodpecker and the Eskimo curlew they are the rarest. The curlew was considered extinct until 1945, but since then has been noted on three occasions in Rockport and Galveston. The ivory-billed woodpecker may be extinct. It was last reported in 1971 in Louisiana.

The waterway was lined with birds of many species. There were oyster catchers with big red bills, and Louisiana herons with feathers of red, white, and blue. Great blue herons lined both banks, erect and motionless, as if supervising the yellowlegs, long-billed curlews, reddish egrets, pintails, and mottled ducks that fed in the waters below. Overhead, three kinds of gulls plied to and fro, and four varieties of terns, Caspian, royal, gull-billed, and Forster's. A large flock of black skimmers rested on a sandbar.

Wild Turkey and Caracara

The Aransas National Wildlife Refuge's 47,000 acres are 45 miles north of Rockport and 75 miles north of Corpus Christi. The area's bays, tidal flats, salt marshes, and higher ground are broken by long, narrow ponds or swales. On the low ridges are the live oaks and sweet-bay bush, leaning permanently away from the gulf winds.

Our first visit to the refuge was by motorcar, and the first objective the tower from which visitors generally look for the whooping cranes. Two to four of the birds could sometimes be seen feeding at a considerable distance. We spotted two, and this was our very first view of these splendid creatures.

On the 5-mile drive from headquarters to the tower we came upon a flock of 20 wild turkeys across the road, including two regal males. On a body of water called Burgentine Lake we sighted thousands of snow geese, while within a few feet of us three cinnamon teal dabbled in the water. We had several fine views of caracaras, vulturelike hawks that are sometimes called Mexican eagles. Avocets also lent interest to the scene.

The refuge's checklist shows 279 species, and the population of individual species is impressive. In one live oak we saw approximately 300 cedar waxwings. Loggerhead shrikes and mockingbirds seemed to appear every few feet of our way.

White-tailed Kite

Much of our birding was done around Rockport on the Gulf, Bayside, and on the way to Sinton. This is a vast agricultural area, chiefly cotton, laced with farm roads that are called shell roads if they are of that composition. Although we were disappointed at missing the mountain plover and Sprague's pipit, we found a compensating reward in a white-tailed kite. This rare species was hawking over a plowed field on our way to Sinton, and was immediately distinguishable by its long, pointed wings and white tail. We have seen the Mississippi kite in Texas and the swallow-tailed kite in Florida, but have never gone searching the Everglades kite at Lake Okeechobee.

In another area we found 56 little brown cranes, a subspecies of the sandhill crane, a few blue geese, and many snow and Canada geese. We tried to get into the new Welder Wildlife Refuge at Sinton, but found that it was open only one day a week, Thursday. It is desirable to phone for an appointment.

Behind our cottage in Rockport we found a flock of 20 pine siskins—this was late in January—and were surprised to see this northern bird in such a low latitude. As we drove along the edge of Aransas Bay in the vicinity of Rockport, we noted thousands of pintails, redheads, and widgeons.

At a place called Rattlesnake Point, we found eight roseate spoonbills, busily feeding by swishing their flat, spoonlike bills side to side under the water.

Connie Hagar

One of our first moves when we settled at Rockport was to call on Mrs. Jack A. Hagar, affectionately known as Connie to innumerable birders across the country. She was the high priestess of bird lore in this area. When we saw her she was 78, and restricted in her activities. She had lived at Rockport since 1935. Mrs. Hagar had compiled a list of approximately 500 species and subspecies of the birds of the central coast of Texas. She discovered numerous rarities, and demonstrated that species previously considered scarce or absent along the Texas coast were actualy regular and sometimes common migrants. She earned the confidence of professional ornithologists to the extent that one of the most cautious of them wrote: "If Connie Hagar reported a great auk in her front yard, I'd believe her!" We found her a bright lady with a nimble wit who that very day was looking forward to giving a talk in Corpus Christi on "The Birds of My Area."

Galveston

On our first family trip to Texas we entered from the west, after leaving Carlsbad Caverns in New Mexico, where we had seen the evening flight of some 4 million free-tailed bats, and followed the Pecos River into Texas. We drove through some rather pleasing country called the Stockton Plateau and the Edwards Plateau. At Ozona, where we slept one night, we found numerous scissor-tailed flycatchers among the trees, along with a pair of Bullock's orioles. The fiery orange and black of the male makes him one of our most spectacular species.

I considered the last day of this month of birding in the West the best. It was spent at Galveston in September, where I had first gone birding by myself in February the previous year. Galveston Island is a barrier beach that lies between the Gulf of Mexico and Galveston Bay. It includes freshwater ponds, marshes, meadows, and miles of shoreline.

We had no sooner turned off the causeway down the road that runs the length of the island than we came to a pond that was liberally sprinkled with birds. Nearest us were long-billed curlews and wading along the grassy shores were reddish, snowy, and common egrets, and Louisiana herons. On the opposite side there was a long line of pink that proved to be 21 roseate spoonbills. We had hoped to find the spoonbills, but local bird watchers told us there was small chance, as the birds had gone south after breeding. Spoonbills are almost 3 feet long, pink in color, heronlike in appearance.

The island held other surprises. In an extensive marsh we

found many other herons, including black- and yellow-crowned night herons, and some three dozen white ibises. This ibis is more than 2 feet long, with pure white plumage relieved only by black wing tips and red face, bill, and legs. The bill is long and down-curved. The island was thronged with other birds, including black-necked stilts, willets, scissor-tailed flycatchers, horned larks, and many other species—truly an amazing place. There was a short-eared owl on a fence in front of our car.

We cannot visit Texas often enough, for there you can see the greatest number of new birds in the shortest time. Three-fourths of all known American species are found in the state, and the Rio Grande Valley is the only place in the nation where such species as white-fronted doves, chachalacas, and green jays may be observed.

5

PACIFIC FLYWAY

Rhinoceros auklet in Strait of Juan de Fuca; Life in the rain forest on Olympic Peninsula; Rich birdlife at Twentynine Palms and Salton Sea; Yosemite and its life zones; From Grand Canyon to Nogales and the high Chiricahuas.

What can you say in only one chapter about birds of the Pacific Flyway? I have touched upon the Olympic Peninsula, and upon exciting places in California, as Twentynine Palms, the Salton Sea, Yosemite, and the area around San Francisco. I have not mentioned other spots we have enjoyed, as the area of hummingbirds southeast of Santa Monica in Los Angeles, the birds on the way to and at Catalina Island, nor Tortilla Flat in the Superstition Mountains past Phoenix. The most grievous omission is the birds of Colorado, which Priscilla likes better than any other state. There at 12,000 feet we found the white-tailed ptarmigan, and many another new species on the intervening slopes.

The Strait at Washington

When in the State of Washington we found that bird watching and salmon fishing go well together. In Port Angeles, we hired a fisherman to take us out into the Strait of Juan de Fuca so we could watch the water birds. The Strait is between the northern shore of Washington and Victoria Island in Canada, and flows from Puget Sound into the Pacific. I was in the region because I had invitations to address the advertising clubs in Seattle and Tacoma.

There happened to be two extra fishing rods on board, and we used them to catch three fine silver salmon, 4 and 11 and 13 pounds. We took the fish to Port Angeles, where two were sent packed in dry ice to our home in New Jersey and the largest to the chairman of my publishing firm in Evanston, Illinois, where it was smoked and relished at a later sales meeting in Lac du Flambeau, Wisconsin. There are facilities in Port Angeles that will process your catch, in small cans with your name on the labels, and these may be used as gifts.

The strait is 20 miles wide, and across from us in Port Angeles was Vancouver Island. We were told that the strait was better for ocean birds than the sound, so while we manned the fishing rods we also kept our binoculars around our necks.

There was much to see. There were two species that were new to us, the common murre (*Uria aalge californica*) and the marbled murrelet. Both are black-and-white birds, somewhat ducklike in appearance; the former is larger and some 17 inches long. They are great divers, and feast upon the herring that throng the waters of the strait.

We saw the hawklike parasitic jaegers pursue gulls and terns to make them disgorge their food. This was the first time we had been close enough to these jaegers to observe the pointed central tail feathers. We chugged past phalaropes riding the waves, and had many close views of surf and white-winged scoters. The dominant cormorant was the Baird's or pelagic cormorant, which is smaller than the Brandt's, also abundant.

After returning to Port Angeles, we drove east to Ediz Hook, a curving strip of land that cuts deeply into the strait from Port Angeles. Since the herring were running close to the shore, we found it rewarding to sit on the great gray logs of spruce and fir that are the driftwood, and to watch the birds prey upon the schools of fish nearby.

Rhinoceros Auklet

In these observations we discovered the rhinoceros auklet, the bird that headed the list of those we most wanted to find on this Western journey. It is a dark, neckless-looking seabird that is approximately 15 inches long. It gets its name from a little horny projection on the upper mandible. The birds nest in colonies on islands off the coast of Washington. This was our first auklet. Later, in Alaska, we found the crested, least, and parakeet auklets.

Gulls were impressive, too. The dominant species was the glaucous-winged gull, somewhat larger than the herring gulls, but lacking the latter bird's black wing tips. A species new to us was the short-billed, or mew, gull. We called it the baby-faced gull because its facial expression was ingenuous, like that of a plover, rather than cynical, like that of a herring gull. The Heermann's, herring, Western, and California gulls abounded, as did the Bonaparte's gull. The last liked to play in the little waves along the shore.

Olympic Peninsula

We drove westward to the Olympic Peninsula, and where we stopped the mountains came down to the ocean, but towering above all was Mt. Olympus, whose glaciers and permanent snowfields we photographed from Hurricane Ridge. The ridge is a mile high, its peak covered with mountain meadows and low evergreen forests. The mountainsides and valleys are blanketed with Alaska yellow cedar, Western hemlock, Douglas fir, and Sitka spruce.

At one place in the ascent we met a band of gray jays, called Oregon jays in that region, that alighted on Priscilla's head and hands, begging food. On the crest of the ridge we found flocks of Savannah sparrows and Oregon juncos, a reddish-brown species with rusty sides. Everywhere we went on the mountains we found golden-crowned kinglets.

Rain Forest

We continued westward, and arrived at Forks on the Pacific. This spot is said to be the wettest community in the United States, with 144 inches of precipitation a year, most of it rain. This moist and mild climate, characteristic of the Pacific side of the Olympic Peninsula, has produced growth that resembles a tropical rain forest. This was the end of September, and, as we signed the register at the motel, we saw that a couple who had signed the day before were a Mr. and Mrs. Cyrus Smythe of Caldwell, New Jersey, our own hometown. We had not known them, but when we returned home got in touch, and subsequently became firm friends.

We explored the rain forest along the Hoh River and found it fascinating. It is a quiet, dimly lighted world, permeated with a misty green light, and yet the bottom of the forest appears luminous in spite of the dense canopy of trees. This is because the light is diffused, reflected from the mosses, vine maples, and all the other greenery on the forest floor. The trees were enormous, the most characteristic being the Sitka spruce, which reaches its greatest size in the Hoh forest. Here there is the largest such tree on record, 51 feet 6 inches in circumference. Another distinctive tree is the Douglas fir, which, with the exception of the sequoia in California, is the largest tree in the Western Hemisphere.

Moss-covered vine maples form an understory beneath the massive conifers, and big-leaf maple, red alder, and cottonwood grow along the river banks. Seventy species of mosses carpet the forest and adorn tree trunks and fallen trees. Many kinds of ferns mingle with the mosses. A mosslike plant forms curtains on the undersides of tree limbs; it is a relative of the ferns and is called Oregon selaginella.

Fallen trees play a unique role in the Olympic rain forest. They become nurseries for a new generation of Sitka spruce and Western hemlock, and are called nurse trees. Tree seedlings that cannot compete with the ground plants can survive on the moist, rotting logs.

The rain forest world has its mammals and birds. It is the home of herds of Roosevelt elk. We saw the Douglas squirrel that feeds on the Douglas fir seed. We found pileated woodpeckers, blue grouse, and gray jays.

Water Ouzel

On the way from Forks to Cape Flattery we passed a mountain stream that became a waterfall. Crawling up the steep face of the rock beside the fall there was a dark, slate-colored bird that we recognized as the dipper, or water ouzel. The bird disappeared over the crest of the fall, but we found it along the stream of the upper side, and were able to observe it closely and take pictures.

The dipper is an amazing bird. It is allied to both the thrushes and wrens, but is the only perching bird that can walk under water. It propels itself with its wings along the bottoms of swift mountain streams, feeding upon insects and fish spawn. It is rather like a chunky wren, but the size of a large thrush. We were startled to hear the bird sing a varied refrain that was something like that of a wren and a bit like that of a Swainson's thrush. We were also impressed to see the bird's shining white eyelids.

On the ocean side of the peninsula is the little Indian village of Lapush. It is a spectacular area, with the Pacific boiling around rocky islands and washing a rocky beach strewn with great logs whitened by the waves. All is against a background of evergreen forests. The ocean was thronged with Western grebes and red-throated loons, and the islands were crowded with cormorants. In the coniferous forests we found sizable flocks of red crossbills and pine siskins.

On the way to Cape Flattery, the farthest west of any spot in the Lower 48, we passed a little valley where Vaux's swifts threaded the air; this is a small dark bird that seems almost to lack a tail. We found ravens and sooty shearwaters at Cape Flattery, but no tufted puffins.

Twentynine Palms and the Salton Sea

One winter day the telephone in my New York office rang and the operator said that Los Angeles was calling. It turned out to be Doug Anderson, who wanted to know if I would discuss the future of advertising before his Western States Advertising Agencies Association in convention at Palm Springs in April.

"We will pay all your expenses," he said, "and please bring Mrs. Barton along." Priscilla had mentioned only the day before the beauty of the deserts in April, and how wonderful it would be to revisit some of the places in California and the Southwest that we had found fascinating two years before.

We flew to Los Angeles the following April, but because of a delay of nine hours in Detroit, missed our plane connection to Palm Springs. We took a plane that flew us to Thermal instead, a dark and dismal place where only one other person got off, but we found a cab to take us to Palm Springs at a cost of fifteen dollars. There we picked up a rented car to drive to our first overnight stay, a motel in Twentynine Palms. This must have been around 11 P.M.

This spot is the headquarters of Joshua Tree National Monument, an area of 1,344 square miles of sand and mountains that lies partly in the Mohave and partly in the Colorado deserts.

One of the main purposes of the monument is to preserve the tall yuccas known as Joshua trees, as well as the other unique animal and vegetable forms of this part of the desert. This is high desert, as the monument runs from 1,000 feet in its eastern part to 5,000 feet in the Little San Bernadino Mountains. Joshua trees are a form of yucca that grows up to 40 feet. They were named by the Mormons, because of the prayerlike attitude of the plant's outstretched arms. Gila woodpeckers live in them, and in abandoned woodpecker holes the little elf owls make their homes. These owls are no larger than sparrows.

Oasis at Twentynine Palms

Two best places for birds in the monument are the oases at Twentynine Palms and Cottonwood Springs, the latter on the southern edge of the monument. The first place was busy with birds, the creatures nesting in the great California palms or feeding among the cottonwoods, mesquite, and creosote bushes. Scores of purple finches made the oasis resound with their lovely warbles, while the Gambel's quail scurried among the underbrush, uttering a loud call that sounded like *kway-o.* Most active of all the birds were the black, silky flycatchers, called phainopeplas. Elegantly crested birds, the size of an oriole, they fed on the mistletoe that grew in reddish clusters on the mesquite bush.

We saw our first roadrunner there. On this very early trip we added four new birds to our life lists in this oasis alone—the Townsend's warbler, verdin, gray vireo, and eared grebe. It is almost unbelievable to find the grebe, a water bird, in such an arid spot as Twentynine Palms. However, there had been a severe storm the week before, and two of the birds had been blown off their migratory course and plumped down in the sands. The grebe is a bird like the loon that cannot take off in flight from land, but has to aquaplane along the surface of the water. The birds had been brought to the ranger in charge of the oasis and he placed them on a small pond there, but the pond was so tiny that it did not give them room to take off, so they seemed destined to be prisoners forever unless the ranger could get them to a larger body of water.

Flowers and Birds

As you drive across the desert in spring to the oasis at Cottonwood Springs you pass through masses of wildflowers, some growing close to the desert floor, some high on the ocotillos, a tall, slim form of plant that is also called desert whip. The ocotillo bears both thorns and dense clusters of bright red blossoms that are attractive to hummingbirds. Among the ocotillos we found two species of hummers we had never seen before, the Costa's and rufous hummingbirds. The first has a bright purple throat and the rufous hummingbird a throat of iridescent red. Cottonwood Springs was also busy with birds, including ladder-backed woodpeckers.

John Hilton's paintings of ocotillo and the oasis at Twentynine Palms are superb, although I did not see them until some time later at the Grand Central Art Galleries in New York. He has a technique that mixes beeswax with his oil paints, and this gives a soft, almost luminous quality to his paintings.

Charles Adams, the ranger at Twentynine Palms, had compiled a list of 180 birds observed in the area of the monument. We found 30 of them the day we spent in the desert there. Sixty or more of the Ranger's birds are purely accidental, as the white pelican, snow goose, common loon, and, of course, the eared grebe.

A vast delight in this country is the flowers; they are especially lovely in the high desert in April and early May. The paloverde, mesquite, ironwood, and other flowering trees are covered with blue and yellow blooms. The bushes are also decked in flowers, the greasewood, tamarisk, and many other varieties. But it is the desert floor that holds the most surprise. White, blue, yellow, and magenta petals are borne by cactus, verbena, lupine, desert marigold, and prickly poppy. It is hard to believe that a grim land can hold such a palette of beauty.

Palm Springs

Palm Springs is a place that is to California what White Sulphur Springs and Hot Springs are to Virginia and the Carolinas. It lies at the foot of Mt. San Jacinto, and the water from mountain lakes supports green lawns and great masses of flowers. The Oasis Hotel, where we put up, is built around and is surrounded by lovely gardens, where the mockingbirds sang all night. The part of the hotel where we slept was covered with espaliered pyracantha. From our veranda one day we saw a Calaveras warbler, similar to our Nashville, and in the streets below the Chinese spotted dove.

Outside the city there are three canyons that are green and rewarding to bird watchers. We visited one, Andreas Canyon, where a lively stream tumbled down the mountain through a setting of palms and gigantic rocks. We found a new bird there, the Lawrence's goldfinch, as well as many familiar species that included the Western bluebird, Abert's towhee, and the magnificent hooded oriole. Near the small stream we found and photographed an unusual orchid, *Epipactis helleborine,* but when we returned we saw that some picnickers had dug it up and put it in a tomato can.

Imperial Valley

After we left Palm Springs, where on the last night we were taken nightclub-hopping by our hosts, we drove southward 50 miles or so, passing through the date-palm groves of Indio and the Coachella Valley, before we sighted the Salton Sea. We went another 50 miles along the landlocked sea and almost to the Mexican border before reaching Brawley, the head of the Imperial Valley and our best place to find a good bed and meal. We discovered by chance an excellent restaurant, hard by our motel, that we have recommended to our friends, and they have concurred. The steak was superb, and the dry Manhattan cocktails are not surpassed by any served in New York.

We wanted to visit this area because it lies on the main migratory lane of northbound birds. The flocks from Mexico stream up the Imperial Valley and skirt the Salton Sea, then follow the Little San Bernadino Mountains to Twentynine Palms. There the migrants split into two groups, proceeding along the eastern and western flanks of the Sierra Nevadas.

The Salton Sea was formed early in the century when the Colorado River overflowed as the result of attempts to divert its waters for irrigation. When the break in the bank was closed, a vast lake was left in a depression that had been known as the Salton Sink. The present Salton Sea covers some 600 square miles, is 40 feet deep, and 270 feet below sea level. Its salinity is somewhat greater than that of ocean water, resulting from the high salt content of the land under both the sea and the water which drains into it.

Alamo River

This is naturally a desert area, whose bleakness is relieved by the irrigated fields of the Imperial Valley. The two best places for birding are both off Route 111, the first being the State Game Refuge along the Alamo River and the other the Salton Sea National Wildlife Refuge. Incidentally, a close friend, Dr. Adrian Sabety of Montclair, New Jersey, who owns thousands of hectares of land in Iran which he has been trying to convert into sugar-beet culture, visited the Imperial Valley to study how sugar beets were grown there and the machinery that was used. He took back to Iran some agricultural machinery specialists from this country to inspect his own cultivation and to recommend other machines.

Flooded grassy meadows along the Alamo were literally teeming with exciting species of birds. In one field we came upon a score of bronze-black creatures as big as medium-sized herons. They had long, down-curved bills and the white border around the base of the bill that gives the white-faced glossy ibis its name. The air was alive with three kinds of swallows, and fluttering among them were handsome black terns. Black-necked stilts waded delicately around the rims of little pools, and swimming in one was a female Wilson's phalarope, in full breeding plumage, much more attractive than the male. The rich chestnut, black, white, and gray of this swimming snipe make it the most beautiful of shorebirds. Curlews and long-billed dowitchers fed with the other birds.

Other parts of the refuge contain a river and a lake and offered an exceptional variety and number of birds. There were four additional kinds of terns, five species of gulls, cormorants, avocets, eared and pied-billed grebes, shovelers and pintails, rails and gallinules. The refuge also has dry fields and wide areas of paloverde, mesquite, and catclaw. In this terrain we found the cactus wren, solitary vireo, and roadrunner, with other land species.

Salton Sea Refuge

The road that turns off Route 111 and leads to Salton Sea National Wildlife Refuge is bordered by canals and irrigation ditches. In the earth piled beside the ditches we saw the tunnels of burrowing owls, and came upon five of the birds either standing at the entrances to their burrows or perched on posts or fence rails. This little owl is slightly larger than a robin, is diurnal in its habits and friendly in its mien. The owl suffers from earthquakes that shatter its tunnels. The Salton Sea is situated almost on top of a fault in the earth's crust that causes most of the quakes along the Pacific Coast. There had been a series of severe shocks just a few days before our arrival, and we could see wide cracks in the roads and dikes.

The 39,000-acre federal refuge around the Salton Sea is also unbelievably rich in birdlife. In one place we found 200 or more white pelicans, while across the marshes we sighted scurrying flocks of cinnamon and green-winged teal. Avocets, sandpipers, curlews, herons, egrets, and various kinds of ducks crowded marshes, mud flats, and shallows. The sea itself was dotted with ducks and grebes. In one spot we found a bush that harbored five shrikes, and in another bush there were seven Brewer's sparrows, a small gray species typical of the desert.

One exciting find was the gull-billed tern, which breeds at Salton Sea, but wanders widely in many parts of the world, occasional vagrants appearing at Brigantine National Wildlife Refuge in New Jersey. It is larger than a common tern, and is distinguished chiefly by its stout, almost gull-like black bill.

This trip produced eleven new birds for our life lists and gave us better acquaintance with species we had known only casually, such as the fulvous tree duck, cinnamon teal, yellow-headed blackbird, and phainopepla. It was also a memorable experience to see both the birds and the flowers in the high and low deserts in the spring.

Yosemite National Park

One summer we camped for several days in Yosemite Valley. In the morning the Steller's jays, black-headed grosbeaks, and Western robins came to our camp table for crumbs, and at night the wind whined through the lofty pines and firs, and black bears raided our food supply.

One night bears tossed our refrigerator around, but could not get it open. However, they thoroughly mixed eggs and milk with vitamin pills. We believe there was one bear and two cubs. Next day we put the food in a carton and hoisted it into a tree, but that was no problem for the bears. We saw them dragging the carton across the road before we were able to chase them away. One of our fellow campers said that a tried system was to mix some gasoline with red pepper and spread this over the tree trunk. I did this, and around two o'clock next morning heard a commotion and a whine, and we assumed the bears had been irritated by the gasoline and pepper mixture. At any rate, we had no more trouble.

There is no space to write of the ponderous masses of granite, such as El Capitan and Half Dome, or of the giant sequoias, unbelievably big and old. But for the birder, especially if he is from the East, there is fascinating interest in the wide variety of species that may be observed. The range of birdlife is accounted for by the different life zones through which one passes in climbing from the San Joaquin Valley, which is practically at sea level, to Tuolumne Meadows and some of the higher peaks where the altitude is 13,000 feet and more.

Life Zones of Yosemite

One theory of the distribution of birds, mammals, and plants is the so-called life-zone system. This is based upon the conception of occurrence of similar organic life in areas or zones where like climate prevails. These zones may occur latitudinally, as across the Arctic or across Canada or across the southern part of the United States, or they may occur altitudinally, as on mountain slopes.

These life zones are not apparent to any great extent in New Jersey, which is primarily a coastal state, but they are impressively evident in Yosemite. In an airline distance of 70 miles, between the western foothills and the crest of the Sierras, changes occur in types of birds and plants that are similar to those found over the 2,000 miles that stretch between our southern states and the arctic tundra. Joseph Wood Krutch in his *The Voice of the Desert* says that the most striking illustration of life zones is found on Mt. San Jacinto near Palm Springs. The eastern slope is so steep that 8,000 feet of altitude is gained in only three linear miles, so that ecologically one travels nearly 5,000 miles while actually climbing only three. "To travel a thousand feet upward is, so far as climate is concerned, the approximate equivalent of traveling 600 miles northward."

As we left Merced, which is in the San Joaquin Valley, and drove the 81 miles to Yosemite, we passed through the so-called Lower Sonoran zone. This is from sea level to 500 feet. It is characterized by grassland with scattered valley oaks. Along the road we stopped at one place to see mockingbirds, a black-necked stilt, killdeer, greater yellowlegs, and Allen's hummingbird, similar to the Eastern red-throated species.

Between 500 and 4,000 feet lies the Upper Sonoran zone. This is the brushland or chaparral area of the foothills, marked by scrub and other species of oaks. While passing through this zone we saw at one spot brown towhees scratching for food in the shadow of an oak, while within a dozen feet of them were lark sparrows and purple finches. We also found the California thrasher there, the Western bluebird, and the California quail.

The transition zone lies between 4,000 and 7,000 feet. The floor of Yosemite Valley is 4,000 feet in elevation. Ponderosa pine, Douglas fir, black oak, and sugar maple are the dominant trees. Near our tent in the mornings we heard the solitary vireo singing in the high trees, and saw its yellow underparts and conspicuous white spectacles. Here also we found the band-tailed pigeon and the water ouzel.

So, as you climb through the other three life zones in Yosemite, the Canadian, Hudsonian, and Arctic-Alpine (Boreal) zones, you find distinctive plants and birds. The Clark's nutcracker and mountain bluebird are found only in the Hudsonian zone where the whitebark pine and mountain hemlock abound, and the other birds and plants are found only in their distinctive life zones.

Point Lobos

When we reached the Pacific Coast we explored some country that is rich in birdlife, including the area along the Pacific Coast from Monterey south to Big Sur State Park; the region at the southern end of San Francisco Bay, likely spots along the Santa Clara Valley, where it was 105 degrees in the shade, the east side of the bay, including marshes and flats, and also the hills of Oakland and Berkeley, and the shores, marshes, ponds, and redwood forests across the Golden Gate to the north of San Francisco.

Black Oystercatchers

Point Lobos Reserve State Park in Monterey County along the south shore of Carmel Bay is an area of 350 acres that is spectacular. Point Lobos has been called "the greatest meeting of land and water in the world." The mountains slide steeply into the Pacific, and their great headlands and granite islands are lashed by the mighty tides of the ocean. This area was called "Point of the Sea Wolves" by the early Spanish, because of the Steller and California sea lions that inhabit the offshore islands. We saw only one of the brutes, but I could hear the others roaring through the fog that enshrouded their islands. Here is one of the few remaining natural groves of Monterey cypress, the trees clinging precariously to the cliffs above the surf, some standing with foliage rich green, others with their weather-worn boughs stark in silhouette.

At one point the shores were busy with a dozen black oyster-catchers, mingling with black turnstones and Western gulls. This oystercatcher is similar to the American species that we see along the Jersey shore occasionally at Beach Haven and Tuckerton, but it has no white in its plumage. It does possess the same heavy red bill. The Western gull is smaller than our great black-backed gull.

White Pelicans

Brown pelicans are common enough in the West, but we did not see a white pelican until we reached the eastern end of Dumbarton Bridge, where it crosses the lower end of San Francisco Bay. A large area of flats was owned by a salt company, and hundreds of white pelicans sunned themselves on the land or sailed by with head hunched back on shoulders and great flat bill resting on curved neck. The white pelican breeds on inland lakes, while the brown pelican is found along the coast.

We had been told to look for yellow-billed magpies in the Santa Clara Valley, and found the bird without trouble, in a field where some water sprays attracted numerous species. This magpie is quite similar to the black-billed magpie that we first saw in Utah, but it has a yellow bill, whereas the other magpie's bill is black. The latter birds do not venture west of the eastern slope of the Sierras, the yellow-billed bird being the species found in the valleys of central California.

Phalaropes and Avocets

Fortunate is the birder on travel who can have the help of a fellow enthusiast who knows the local scene. That was our good fortune in Oakland, where Howard Cogswell, who taught biological sciences at Mills College, took us in tow.

He showed us the Point Bonita area across the Golden Gate from San Francisco, where many northern and one red phalarope swam in the shallow ponds. The description of the phalarope as a swimming sanderling is an apt one, as the birds are light colored and the same size as sanderlings. There also we found the black phoebe and wren-tit.

Professor Cogswell next took us across the bay to Oakland and showed us one place where an estimated 100,000 Western sandpipers were feeding, along with hundreds of avocets and willets. This was called Bay Farm Island. We left the lowlands and climbed a very dry hill to find the rufous-crowned sparrow. This species is somewhat similar to the chipping sparrow, but always lives on dry hillsides that are covered with low bushes and grasses, the habitat in which we found it. Our daughter, Debby, thirteen, was disappointed in that, instead of visiting the Top of the Mark, she went to Bay Farm Island, which she called a garbage dump.

Another memorable trip was to Muir Woods, a Coast redwood grove named after John Muir. This area produced the pileolated warbler, similar to the Wilson's warbler, the Bewick's wren, and chestnut-backed chickadee.

Grand Canyon

We crossed into Arizona from California by way of Blythe. I had never seen birds so tame as they were at Grand Canyon. As I sat at my camp table, there were dozens of birds feeding on the crumbs I scattered on the ground or exploring the area out of tastes developed from the visits of other campers. Most numerous were robins and chipping sparrows. The chestnut-backed bluebird is somewhat different from our Eastern species. It has a rusty patch on its back. Another attractive and friendly visitor was the pygmy nuthatch. It is very small, smaller even than our red-breasted nuthatch, and almost an inch shorter than our white-breasted species. It liked the pinyon pines and junipers that surrounded the camp, but also visited the camp table.

Also common about the camp were two very similar juncos, the gray-headed and red-backed. Since the elevation of the southern rim of Grand Canyon is some 7,000 feet, it is natural to see there birds that otherwise might be found in the cool latitudes of Canada in September. Both these juncos have ash-gray sides and bright rufous backs. The only difference is in the color of the upper mandible. We were tipped off to this by Louis Shellbach, who had been the naturalist at the Canyon for twenty-two years, and took us to his museum to show us skins of birds native to the area. Many other birds visit the camp or fly by; we were interested especially in the noisy flocks of pinyon jays.

Roadrunner and Phainopepla

Before we started our first Western trip, we placed ten birds on our desired list, those we wanted most to see: water ouzel, wandering tattler, phainopepla, roadrunner, cactus wren, pyrrhuloxia, scissor-tailed flycatcher, vermilion flycatcher, lazuli bunting, and roseate spoonbill. We found eight, missing the pyrrhuloxia and lazuli bunting; this is unusual in the case of the pyrrhuloxia, as the bird is not scarce. We discovered the water ouzel along a brook in Yosemite and by a stream in Washington. The wandering tattler, a medium-sized shorebird, was in the company of black turnstones on the shore of the Pacific in San Francisco. The roadrunner was in an oasis at Twentynine Palms. This is truly a remarkable species. Almost two feet long, the "chaparral cock" is brown, heavily streaked with black. It has a shaggy crest and a long tail, both of which it elevates rhythmically as if expressing some decisive mood. Friends who have visited Tucson recently say the birds run along the tops of houses, since the streets are choked with traffic.

We found the cactus wren not in the great Joshua Tree National Monument, but in a street in Wickenburg. This is a desert town of 2,000 or so population (formerly a gold-mining place), where we spent one night. There we first saw the free-tailed bat. Early in the morning, as we were leaving, we determined to look down the street near our motel.

There, in the space of half an hour, we saw six birds we had never seen before. They were the cactus wren, Say's phoebe, hooded oriole, curve-billed thrasher, white-winged dove, and Gila wood-pecker.

Some of these birds are not rare in the area, but this was our first trip West, when almost every species could have been new. The experience reminds me of a visit we had years later from a young bird bander we met first in Spain. In his career at Oxford, he led an ornithological expedition to Afghanistan, and then secured a position teaching biology at New Mexico State University. He visited us going to and from his new post, and one day we took him birding. He saw 54 species in New Jersey that were completely new to him, because he had never been in our country before. He said this was the single best day of birding in his life, the second best day being one in India.

The phainopepla first occurred in the high country, 50 miles or so south of Grand Canyon. We stopped by the road at a field covered with Utah juniper and noticed considerable bird activity. There was not merely one phainopepla, but half a dozen. This flycatcher is the size of an oriole, a slim, glossy black bird with a crest and noticeable white patches in the wings. In the same field were many lark sparrows, the latter occasionally chasing the larger birds. We had looked the afternoon before for these silky flycatchers on the banks of the Colorado River in a busy town named Blythe. The temperature was 111 in the shade and, as they say in these parts, "six feet above zero" in the sun. Blythe has what they call 365 days of sunshine a year. That means it never rains, except perhaps in leap year.

Approximately 190 species of birds have been found in Grand Canyon. As one goes down the canyon from some 8,000 feet in altitude to near sea level, he passes through four life zones, hence sees birds that would be characteristic of zones from Mexico to Canada.

Everywhere we have gone we have met a heat wave. In Los Angeles there was a succession of days above 100 that broke all records back to the 1800s. And also smog. The only new bird I saw in Los Angeles was a plain titmouse at the Hollywood Bowl.

Phoenix and Tucson

After leaving Grand Canyon we drove to Phoenix and Tucson, where I gave talks before advertising clubs, and proceeded on our journey south and east. From Tucson we visited the San Jose Wildlife Sanctuary, only a dozen miles from Nogales on the Mexican border.

This area is sponsored by the Tucson Audubon Society, is traversed by a pleasant stream, and is covered by trees and other tall vegetation. We saw the vermilion flycatcher here for the first time, a bird as big as a sparrow, with head and underparts of flaming red.

This was the only spot where we found blue grosbeaks. Along the stream green-backed goldfinches sounded their plaintive notes, and in one tree, brooding over the scene and uttering a strange and repeated cry, we found a gray hawk, sometimes called Mexican goshawk, the size of a Cooper's hawk. It is a buteo.

This trip produced 110 new birds for my life list, and my wife, who started earlier, on August 10, had 125. I left on the trip later in the month. There is no space here to tell of all the fascinating places and species. In Phoenix, for instance, we visited Encanto Park early one morning and made the acquaintance of the charming little Inca dove and the Bendire's thrasher and Abert's towhee. Outside of Tucson we spent a morning in Sabino Canyon, noted for its tall saguaro cactus. This visit produced the desert sparrow, distinct in its black throat patch and white face stripes. Nor can I more than mention the white-necked ravens in southeastern New Mexico, birds that are smaller than common ravens and distinguished by white neck feathers that are seen when the wind ruffles them.

We went into Mexican Nogales, just to touch foot on foreign soil, had a slight meal, and thought we could return to the United States as easily as we had returned to our own country from Canada. The U.S. custom officials could not believe, however, that we would have taken our station wagon, two children, and loads of equipment into Mexico for only an hour's stay. They said, "Break it down," so I began to pull our luggage from the rack on top of the car and from the compartment in the station wagon. One suitcase we pulled out was our daughter's, and when they opened it and found it filled with little feminine things, they were probably convinced that we were not running dope, and allowed us to return to our homeland without further search.

After Nogales we went east, first passing through Pearce, an abandoned gold-mining town. Here my wife and daughter asked the way to the outhouse, and found there, instead of a Sears and Roebuck catalog, the most recent Christmas issue of *Punch*. The general store was four-fifths empty, many fences around former residences had been carted away for firewood, and many houses had been torn down for lumber, wood being a scarce commodity in that part of the country.

From Pearce we continued east. We had asked persons in that community how to get over the mountains, and they said to take Onion Saddle road. The Chiricahua Mountains in southeastern Arizona rise abruptly 8,000 feet out of a green and flowered plain. A single-lane dirt road crosses a spot 7,500 feet high called Onion Saddle, and this provided a bit of driving long to be remembered. It was the only time our car was overheated. Fortunately, we met no others on the two-hour climb. If you do, there is something about the driver coming down having the right of way. One of our friends who took the same ride was less fortunate. He was driving up the road and met another coming down. The driver descending stopped, took out a book, and began to read. Our friend, noting that this was a local citizen, figured that he would probably outlast his patience. He asked the local driver how much his car was worth, and was told two hundred and fifty dollars. Our friend wrote a check for that amount, gave it to the local driver, and pushed the car just acquired into the canyon.

Onion Saddle Road

On Onion Saddle Road, on the mountainside, and in the valleys, we found the lovely hepatic tanager, also the bridled titmouse, Arizona jay, green-tailed towhee, Gambel's quail, and Arizona junco. It provided a certain satisfaction to see all the species of one family that may be found in the United States. We can claim this for the towhees, titmice, herons, and egrets, disregarding the possibilities, for instance, of seeing a bird that has been recorded as only accidental, the little egret.

Over the crest we came upon an experimental station maintained by the American Museum of Natural History, and there learned how wild the region actually is. The mountains harbor bears, wolves, cougars, jaguars, and other fierce beasts. I believe this was the first year of the station, but learned that food and board were low priced, and one might have the privilege of staying there if he had a research project of some merit that was approved by the museum. Like other attractive ideas, however, we never had the time to pursue it, although Alexander M. White, president of the museum, was in my class in college.

Carlsbad Caverns

Having crossed the ridge and spent the night in Lordsburg, New Mexico, we proceeded to Carlsbad Caverns. We saw the spectacular flight of bats, as they emerged at night to feed, and someone has estimated they number 4 million. This is the Mexican free-tailed bat, a strange creature that we had first seen in Wickenburg. The tails look longer in life than I have ever seen them in an illustration. We asked one of the rangers about predatory birds, and he said the bats are little troubled because they are more agile than the birds. The red-tailed hawk is not successful in capturing these leathery mammals, although the Cooper's does better. Great horned owls sometimes prey upon bats.

Where shall we go next? Possibly to southern Arizona. On the lower slopes of the southeastern mountains we may find the zone-tailed hawk, the whiskered owl, the Rivoli's and blue-throated hummingbirds, the coppery-tailed trogon, and the rose-throated becard. We may also explore the higher parts of these mountains and seek the red-faced warbler and the flammulated owl.

6

STRANGE BIRDS
IN FAR PLACES

I confess that when we take trips to far places we are more interested in the birds than in the peoples thereof. Our objective is to explore a land that offers most in birds we have not seen or have not seen in their native habitats. On the Gaspé Peninsula we went to see the breeding colonies of gannets, in the Coto de Doñana we sought the flamingos, in Trinidad we found the oilbirds and scarlet ibises. We do not neglect completely the peoples or their cultures, but have found that it is best to have a major objective on a trip, and ours is birds.

ALASKA

Fly down the Aleutians 700 miles from Anchorage, and when you reach Cold Bay turn northwest and proceed another 300 miles over the Bering Sea and you come to Alaska's Pribilof Islands. There are three islands and two rocks, the total some 40 square miles in area. We were accompanied on this trip by two longtime friends, Mary and Will Gilman of Wellesley Hills, Massachusetts. Mary was a classmate of Priscilla's at Radcliffe.

A visit to the largest island, St. Paul, is exciting chiefly for its birds and fur seals. Its colonies of seabirds are the largest in North America, and the rocky cliffs that border the sea provide nesting sites that can be viewed easily from the tundra above. We looked down upon innumerable thick-billed and common murres, clouds of least auklets, and smaller numbers of crested and parakeet auklets. Both the horned and tufted puffins were nesting on the cliffs, sharing rocky sites with black-legged and red-legged kittiwakes, the latter being a species that occurs only in the Pribilofs. Pelagic and red-faced cormorants also crowded the cliffs.

At one spot we saw a small pool among the rocks where a snow bunting and three gray-crowned rosy finches were bathing. This was the first time we had seen the bunting in its beautiful black-and-white summer plumage. We found another pool that had attracted a blue fox. This blue phase of the arctic fox was introduced into the islands after World War I as a source of commercial fur farming, but the pelts are worthless now because of changing fashion, and the creatures eat eggs of colonial seabirds, especially those of murres.

Life on the Tundra

The frozen tundra of the North melts in summer to a depth of a half foot or more. The soft upper area is then covered with flowers, broad masses everywhere of tall blue lupine, bordered and interspersed with yellow arctic poppies. As we walked we came upon a score or more of less conspicuous but equally lovely blossoms. There was forget-me-not, the state flower, with blooms like our familiar species, but growing low in small compact mounds with little leaves. Spring beauty was larger than our more southern species and was pink. Jacob's ladder, beach pea, arctic daisy, lousewort, and violets were other blossoms familiar to us as visitors from the "Lower 48."

As we admired the flowers, we heard birdsong; Lapland longspurs were abundant, and they reminded us of the song of the Western meadowlark. Gray-crowned rosy finches gave their high chirping notes, and glaucous-winged gulls cried from nearby beaches. At several spots we startled rock sandpipers, birds that reminded us of our smaller dunlins, but are native to western Alaska and southeastern Siberia.

Fur Seal Colony

St. Paul and adjacent St. George Island are the only breeding grounds in North America of the northern fur seal. The herd of some 1.5 million is managed by the U.S. Department of the Interior. One of the problems is to prevent overpopulation in this restricted area, hence some of the young bulls are killed each year, the income from their valuable pelts contributing to the Alaskan economy.

St. Paul was a vast sounding board for the roaring bulls. Each breeding bull or beachmaster has an average-sized harem of 36 cows, some more than 75. They and the bachelor seals, the pups, and the discarded old beachmasters live in crowded propinquity on the rocky beaches. The bulls arrive at the Pribilofs early in May from wintering waters off Southern California and Japan, and are joined later by nearly a million females whom the bulls gather into some 8,000 harems. Each bull is vicious and vigilant in protecting his harem from the intrusions of other males and the wanderings of his females. He neither eats nor drinks in the breeding season, and sleeps very little, so after the season is over he is so exhausted that he has to sleep for several days. He may lose 200 pounds in weight. We had no difficulty in getting good photographs with our 400-mm telephoto lens.

Kenai Peninsula

One day while in Anchorage we drove down toward the Kenai Peninsula to see Portage Glacier. It is in the Chugach Mountains, and its melting ice flows into Portage Lake. This lake was formed some fifty-five years ago, but the glacier is melting so much faster than it is forming that in approximately twenty years it will be back out of the lake it excavated in its forward advance. Ice at the edge of the glacier forms spectacular and lovely designs as it breaks off in huge chunks, a process called calving. Some of the ice and water gleam blue, providing an exciting situation for the photographer.

On the way to the glacier we stopped at Mt. Alyeska (2,610 feet) where there is a ski trail. Alyeska is the Indian name from which Alaska was derived, and means the "Big Land." We rode up and down the mountain in the chair lifts, a mile and a quarter each way, and noted the birds in the spruce forests. There were birdsongs we did not know, but we did identify notes of the gray-cheeked thrush, a song that suggests the veery's. On patches of snow below we saw water pipits, and violet-green swallows threaded the air, one pair nesting in the housing of one of the sheaves through which the cable runs that supports the lift. The Gilmans, who ski regularly, enjoy birds in this way in New England in its late springtime.

Mt. McKinley

To see for the first time and in a single day a grizzly bear, moose, caribou, and Dall sheep is an occasion long to remember, but that was our experience on our first day in Alaska's Mt. McKinley National Park. The park is a wilderness area of more than 3,000 square miles, dominated by lofty Mt. McKinley, highest peak on the continent.

On this first day we and a group drove 65 miles into this majestic park through steep mountains. The most impressive creatures we met were the caribou. They appeared in small bands and in herds of as many as 400, moving fluidly across a river valley. Each spring the caribou that have wintered north of the park move into it eastward, crossing the Alaska Range over glaciers at the heads of rivers. After feeding on the south side of the range they return en masse in July, which was when we saw them. At this season herds numbering 1,000 to 2,000 are not unusual.

Moose reach their greatest size in Alaska, a mature bull weighing 1,500 pounds. We saw such a great beast in the willows along one of the mountain passes. Willows are the chief browse food of the moose.

We saw only one grizzly bear, and it was at a safe distance in a valley below our road. The bears are dangerous, and motorists are cautioned to remain in their cars while in bear country. The grizzlies are related closely to the coastal brown bears, called the largest carnivores on earth.

We sighted eight Dall sheep on the side of a mountain. This is the only white mountain sheep in the United States. The horns are never shed, and continue to grow throughout the beast's life-span of eleven to fourteen years. The sheep have an aesthetic appeal, partly because they are associated with their beautiful haunts, the steep cliffs and ledges with their green slopes spangled with flowers.

The two outstanding birds we found in the park were the willow ptarmigan and long-tailed jaeger, both with chicks. The several trails around the park hotel provided numerous orange-crowned and a few Wilson's warblers, gray jays, and magpies.

Stern-wheeler Ride

One day in Fairbanks we rode on one of the last Alaskan stern-wheeler riverboats, going up and down the Chena and Tanana rivers. The Chena is fed by rains, the Tanana by glaciers, hence its water is called "glacier milk," gray and soupy from silt brought down by the ice masses. The banks are bordered by willow, aspen, and birch, and once we stopped at an Indian fishing camp.

We found at the edge of the camp boreal chickadees, brownish birds that visit New Jersey only rarely in the winter. More than half of Alaskan bird species can be found in eastern United States.

Northernmost Point

We flew from Fairbanks over the formidable Brooks Range to Barrow, the most northern community in America. It is 330 miles above the Arctic Circle, the sun never sets for 82 days in summer, and there is no tide. We took a photograph of the midnight sun at F22 and 1/1,000 of a second. Our very modest lodgings were on the shore of the Arctic Ocean, with the near shore ice breaking off continually into icebergs, while farther out and barely visible was the arctic ice pack that never melts. Barrow is some 150 miles west of Prudhoe Bay, site of oil discoveries.

It is a desolate place, where the shacks of the large Eskimo population are surrounded by military junk abandoned after World War II. There are no sidewalks, and a gray volcanic grit covers roads and beaches. There are relatively few sled dogs, because the Eskimos now use snowmobiles.

There are no trees, because this is arctic tundra, whose surface melts only a little before it reaches the permafrost or perennially frozen ground. It is difficult to bury anyone, and the new natural gas pipelines are some four feet above ground. It was very cold in late July, and we wore parkas and boots, furnished by the airline.

Priscilla and I walked over the tundra and found the most noteworthy bird to be the wheatear. It has a blue-gray back, black wings, and flashy black-and-white tail. The wheatear breeds in northern Alaska and winters in the Old World. We had seen it in September in Spain. Also on the tundra were Baird's sandpipers, dunlins, and Lapland longspurs. Snow buntings in their black-and-white summer plumage sang larklike songs. These buntings were also common around the houses and on the streets of the village.

Glacier Bay

Glacier Bay is situated at the northwest end of the Alexander Archipelago, which is in southeastern Alaska. This national monument was established to preserve the spectacle of great glaciers descending from high mountains and calving icebergs into salt water. Absence of roads to the monument limits travel to boats and aircraft.

One day we took a ten-hour boat trip up and down the bay, passing from dense forest to barren glacial outwash, from mud flat to sea cliff and back. We found 20 species of birds in these varied habitats.

Most remarkable were approximately 25,000 northern phalaropes in Sitakaday Narrows. Here, in the so-called rips, almost the entire tidal flow of Glacier Bay is compressed in order to pass a point of land and nearby islands. The resulting turbulence brings marine life close to the surface, where it was furnishing food for gulls, both horned and tufted puffins, phalaropes, murres, and murrelets. These were both marbled and Kittlitz's murrelets, the latter a new species for us.

As we passed Marble and other islands, we noted other species: black oystercatchers, harlequin ducks, pigeon guillemots, white-winged and surf scoters, bald eagles, pelagic cormorants, while arctic and glaucous-winged gulls plied the air.

Preserving Specimens

When I was at the University of Alaska I was impressed by a display of birds that were preserved and mounted in a wonderfully natural way. The specimens included boreal owl, Swainson's thrush, redpoll, and myrtle warbler. Small mammals were also in the display.

As the university described the new technique, the fresh bird and mammal specimens are frozen in sealed plastic bags and shipped to the taxidermist in dry ice. They are then thawed, placed in a natural position, supplied with artificial eyes, and refrozen at −5 degrees Fahrenheit.

After a few days the specimen is removed and placed in a freeze-dry apparatus, which consists basically of a freezing chamber connected to a vacuum pump and a condenser. Under low temperatures in a vacuum, water is actually pulled from the tissues of the specimens with a minimum of shrinkage. After several weeks, the specimen is removed in the finished form.

I cannot do justice to Alaska in a few pages. It is such a large and fascinating land that I can mention only some of the other rewarding trips we took, as to Kotzebue, a large Eskimo community; to Nome; a railroad trip from Skagway to Lake Bennett on the White Pass and Yukon Railroad that follows the old trail taken in 1898 by stampeders rushing to the Yukon gold fields. The 12-mile-long Mendenhall Glacier near Juneau was a memorable experience. Nor can I mention all the unusual birds we saw: the white wagtail at Lake Bennett, the Aleutian tern at Kotzebue, the sharp-tailed sandpiper on the shore of Knick Arm at Anchorage.

We saw 106 species of birds in three weeks in Alaska, 28 new to us. But the trip provided also an insight into a frontier society, an acquaintance with Eskimo and Indian communities, and an enjoyment of unsurpassed natural beauty.

TRINIDAD

We had long wanted to see the oilbirds that live in caves in Trinidad, as well as the wealth of tropical birdlife to be found elsewhere on that island, so one snowy day in December we left Pittstown and flew to Port of Spain, arriving at 4 A.M. The plane was five hours late, but our driver was still waiting, and took us 15 miles over a road that rose tortuously at times to 1,200 feet in the Northern Range of mountains. Our destination was the Asa Wright Nature Center in Arima, a mecca for birders from faraway places.

Mr. and Mrs. Wright came from Cornwall, England, in 1947, to buy for Mr. Wright some 200 acres and a large house at this asthma-free spot in a tropical rain forest. The place is called Spring Hill, and its main commercial crop was cocoa. However, grapefruit, oranges, and bananas also abound. After her husband's death, Mrs. Wright began to accommodate birders, as the estate's fame for its birdlife began to spread, an interest that was kindled by studies done there by William Beebe. In 1968 Mrs. Wright sold the plantation, and through the contributions of friends and naturalists, a nature center was formed in a trust with a Canadian bank. She was a remarkable woman, with a Viking ancestry. Mrs. Wright herself died in 1971. Many of our friends have visited Spring Hill, and outstanding naturalists such as Peter Scott, Jacques Berlioz, and Don Eckelberry.

Oilbirds at Spring Hill

Oilbirds somewhat resemble nightjars, although they are in a family of their own. They are surprisingly large, with a length of

17 inches and a wingspread of 3 feet. Their upper plumage is grayish brown, glossed with pinkish cinnamon. Lower plumage is pale cinnamon-buff. The bill is powerfully hooked, and deep chestnut bristles almost two inches long protrude from the area of the beak. The bird feeds on fruits of many kinds of trees, including palms. This diet makes them so fat that in other times their bodies were rendered by the local residents to provide oil for lamps. Hence the name oilbird. An additional advantage of the oil is that it is slow to turn rancid.

We climbed a rugged and slippery trail to a deep chasm in the rocks through which the Arima River flows. We followed the river in water almost knee deep and through rocks to the walls on which the birds were nesting. When disturbed by our torch they made loud noises like those produced by a ratchet. When they flew from their nests, they were awesome in the gloom with their thin large-sized bat appearance and red eyes seen clearly after the beam was thrown upon them. This colony numbered 38. Around the nests grew in the dim light stunted palms from seeds dropped by the birds.

Three Thousand Scarlet Ibises

We went to Caroni Swamp, an hour's drive from Arima, to see the scarlet ibises. This is a mangrove swamp of some 60 square miles that contains four sanctuaries with lakes and canals that thread the dense growth. Our boatman, who knew the birds well, took us to one lake in late afternoon as the ibises were flying in to roost. The flocks of gorgeous birds against the blue sky or on the dark mangroves on the islands where they roost provided an unforgettable sight.

There were some 3,000 scarlet ibises roosting on the lake, with the population of the whole swamp estimated at around 10,000, a large increase since the birds have been protected. Roosting in the same trees were snowy and cattle egrets, little blue, common, and Louisiana herons. There was also the cocoi heron, similar to our great blue.

While boating on the lake or along the canals we came upon other noteworthy species. There was a pair of prothonotary warblers and two kinds of tyrant flycatchers, black-and-white birds that bear the engaging local names of white-shouldered washerwoman and white-headed widow. An unusual bird was the white-barred bush shrike, one of the antbirds. Antbirds do not always eat ants, and the bush shrike merely follows army ants and feeds upon insects that the ants flush. It is the size of a sparrow, its entire plumage black and white, striped on the head and throat, barred on the rest of the body, wings, and tail.

There was also the peppershrike, a species in a subfamily of the vireos. It, too, is sparrow-size, an olive-brown bird with gray cheeks and chestnut-brown eyebrows, whose song is a variable tune of whistled notes. Its food is insects and other invertebrates. A spectacular species was the yellow oriole, the size of our Baltimore oriole, but rich golden yellow with black throat, wings, and tail. On the return trip at dusk along the canals we saw two large birds that were potoos or giant nightjars.

Nariva Swamp

Another trip, with a driver who was a splendid birder with telescopic eyes, took us to a swamp along the Nariva River and to Manzanilla Beach in the eastern part of the island. On the way we stopped at Waller Field, a former U.S. Air Force installation, and in the surrounding savannah found among other species several jacanas, which walk on the lily pads; red-breasted marsh birds, which are blackbirds with red breasts; glossy grassquits, tiny blue-black birds that have the peculiar habit of flying vertically upward from a perch for a foot or more and then returning to the precise spot, and ruddy ground doves.

Manzanilla Beach is picturesque and smooth, bordered with palms. We drove for miles without seeing a person on the sands. Magnificent frigate birds sailed overhead, brown pelicans fished in the waves, and land birds perched along the road. One was the Swainson's pearl kite, a pygmy falcon shorter than a robin, with white, yellow, and plumbeous plumage. Other allied birds of prey we had seen were the black, Brazilian marsh, red-winged, white, and gray hawks. A memorable view was a band of eight blue-and-yellow tanagers, one of 12 kinds of tanagers we were able to identify in Trinidad.

When we walked into Nariva Swamp we came to a 20-acre field known as the Melon Patch, because melons used to be grown there. It was surrounded by palms and other trees, some covered with strangler figs. Flying noisily among the crowns of the palms were some 30 Amazon green parrots, a green-and-yellow species more than a foot long, while in nearby trees green parakeets chattered, as a flock of red-bellied macaws flew by. Gray and tropical kingbirds frequented the area.

On the way to Nariva Swamp we stopped briefly at Sangré Grande to see the smaller cacique, which is also known as the yellow-rump or yellow-backed cornbird. It is related to the grackles, blackbirds, and orioles. This cacique is a bit more than 10 inches long, black with a bright yellow patch on the wing, bright yellow mid-back, rump, and basal part of tail, also under tail coverts. It is noisy and gregarious, building stockinglike nests. It is a half-foot smaller than the yellow-tail or large cornbird that we found common and spectacular at Spring Hill, nesting in colonies in the immortelle trees.

Bellbird

In two weeks in Trinidad we saw 156 species of birds, although we neglected entirely the calypso, steel bands, limbo, and other entertainment in Port of Spain. We did savor island food, however, and one morning on a rural road enjoyed break-fast of wild pig and deer meat in a curry sauce. We ate it between double-decked pancakes flavored with ground peas and spices called roti. One afternoon we stopped for tea at a house where milk and butter came from water buffalo.

Another time we visited Pitch Lake, which provides some 165,000 tons of commercial asphalt a year from its inexhaustible supply. The surface is solid enough to allow trucks to pass over it quickly, but the whole area around the lake is so uncertain because of the subterranean tar that the road over which we drove was rough with troughs although only recently resurfaced. Houses must be light and built of wood, and in some instances were set on rafts. It was said that if you left your motorcar parked too long it would sink so deeply it could not be pulled out.

We went to Arena Forest (so-called because it is sandy, like a bullfighting arena), and found three interesting birds—the bell-bird, leaf-scraper, and Guy's white-tailed hermit. The bellbird is elusive, but we were alerted to its presence by its call, which resembles that produced by hitting an anvil with a hammer. The bird sat quietly in a tall tree; it was nearly 11 inches long, with grayish white plumage, coffee-colored head, and black wings. Its throat was bare, and hanging from it were black, stringlike wattles.

The leaf-scraper is a small brown bird that nests in banks along the road, excavating a tunnel a foot or more long. It is an ovenbird that earns its name by lining its nest with the mid-ribs of leaves from which it has torn the other parts. The hermit is a large hummingbird with an unusually long curved bill. In January and February the birds assemble for singing, hovering around favorite perches and uttering short, loud notes at irregular intervals.

Two of the most striking of tropical birds we found were the toucan and jacamar. The toucan was the sulphur-and-white-breasted variety, and was identified easily by its enormous black bill, heavy and almost 5 inches long. The bird stretches 20 inches, with blue face, black plumage set off by crimson rump, orange-

and-yellow breast, and crimson at the base of the tail. The toucan hops from branch to branch with dexterity, eating fruits and berries. The rufous-tailed jacamar is in a family of its own. An insect eater, it has a long, narrow black bill, white throat, narrow green collar, chestnut underparts, and iridescent green upper parts. As does the leaf-scraper, it nests in a tunnel in a low bank.

Species and Their Names

We were impressed by the many species in a single family of birds. We saw 17 different kinds of flycatchers, 12 varieties of hummingbirds, 12 types of tanagers, 8 species of blackbirds and orioles, 6 kinds of hawks, and 3 varieties of trogons.

The antbirds, manakins, and honeycreepers are quite unlike anything found in temperate climes, as is natural, since Trinidad is only seven miles from Venezuela. Certainly, Trinidad gives one the chance to see tropical birds easily and comfortably, as the mountain areas in January are cool and insect-free, and much of the best birding can be done along the roads.

When we were in Trinidad we found some confusion about the common names of birds. When we returned from a field trip we would ponder until midnight to give correct names to the birds we had seen. The sources we used were *The Birds of Trinidad and Tobago,* by G. A. C. Herklots; the Florida Audubon Society checklist; and a list obtained at Spring Hill of the birds seen there by visiting ornithologists. The Florida Audubon Society list did not include the scientific names. When we returned home, Priscilla and I tried to reconcile these lists by making one that included the scientific names for each bird and all the common names given it by various sources. Where possible we gave preference to common names in the *Species of Middle American Birds,* by Eugene Eisenmann, Transactions of the Linnaean Society of New York, April 1955. We sent our list to Spring Hill for possible use by visitors.

PORTUGAL AND SPAIN

We sat in the sidewalk cafe before the only hotel in the little town of Santiago do Cacem in Portugal and, as we drank a pitcher of the excellent local wine, watched the house martins enter their mud nests. These swallows are common in Europe; they are blue-black above, white beneath, and have a pure white rump. Under the eaves of a nearby house there were a hundred or more nests, enclosed mud structures similar to those of our own cliff swallows.

This was not a resort place, and we and our companions, Rosa and Brice Sumner of Washington, appeared to be the only North Americans there. The men in their black suits and flat-topped black hats and the women in their long black skirts and shawls were mildly curious about our bird watching, but uniformly polite. One night there was a fair on the grounds just to the rear of our hotel. The girls appeared in pretty dresses, and the musicians played the *fado*, a sad, nationally popular type of song.

As we had driven down from Lisbon we passed through dry lands studded with plantations of cork oaks. The cork is stripped from the trees periodically, and we saw wagons and trucks laden with cork pass by. When a tree is stripped it is numbered in white for the year.

The trees attracted numerous birds, among them the great tits. These are small, plump, short-billed birds similar to our chickadees. They are the largest of the common tits in Europe, with glossy, blue-black heads and necks, white cheeks, and yellow underparts. Distinctive is a black band from neck to belly. The swift occurred there, as did the spotted flycatcher and the short-toed tree creeper, similar to our brown creeper.

Westernmost Europe

We drove west of Lisbon, along the Tagus River to Estoril, Cascais, and Sintra. We liked Cascais particularly; its sunny harbor was thronged with fishing boats, over which hovered lesser black-backed and herring gulls and common terns. On one side of the harbor rose steep, rocky cliffs whose crevices provided homes for crag martins, which are somewhat similar to our bank swallows.

From Cascais we took the sea route north to Sintra through scrubby pines and sun-bleached dunes to the rocky spine of the Serra Sintra, passing Cabo da Roca, westernmost point in continental Europe. The way was spectacularly beautiful, looking down on the ocean; colorful houses and estates are on the little slopes, some with windmills. Looking upward we saw stern peaks upon which were perched castles and monasteries. This was a rugged drive, the narrow road along the mountains filled with hairpin turns that did not permit stopping to look for birds. The town of Sintra is on a rocky mass thrust up by a volcanic eruption from which burst hundreds of springs. The ever-verdant land is filled with flowers, including 90 exotic blooming species. Sintra has been a home for most of the kings of Portugal. Among the castles is a ruined Moorish structure, and an ancient monastery is nearby.

Birds in Lisbon

Lisbon is rich in well-kept parks, and we visited one near our hotel in Avenida de Liberdade, which is the Champs Elysées of Lisbon. We strolled through Parque Eduardo VII, and found numerous characteristic species of birds in the mixed deciduous and evergreen vegetation. There were two we had known in England—the robin, a plump little bird with a rich orange breast, and the blackbird, which is a thrush and similar to our American robin except that it is all black. In addition to the spotted flycatcher we saw the pied flycatcher, whose male is bluish above, white below, with a large white area on the wing.

In and around a pond in the park were several exotic species of waterfowl and other birds, the situation reminding us of St. James's Park in London. The species included white storks and flamingos, which are not really exotic, as the stork is found wild in both Portugal and Spain, and the flamingo occurs in the southern parts of Spain and France.

Coto de Doñana

Our first city in Spain was Huelva, which is across the river that divides southern Portugal from Spain. It was a scary crossing, in a small boat with planks running from the vessel to the dock and over these I had to drive the car. At Huelva we rested a few days and bought provisions for our stay at the Coto de Doñana.

The Coto is an area adjacent to the great Las Marismas marshes in southwestern Spain. We saw 102 species of birds there, of which the rarest was the lesser-short-toed lark and most impressive the Spanish imperial eagle. A spectacular sight was 450 or more flamingos on a remote laguna, in the company of spoonbills, avocets, black-winged stilts, and numerous other species of shorebirds.

Called the most important wildlife sanctuary in Europe, the Coto de Doñana is higher and drier than the bordering marshes. The Marismas are situated where the great Rio Guadalquivir divides southwest of Seville into several channels before joining again to enter the Atlantic. These are said to be the largest brackish marshes on the continent, covering some 450 square miles.

The Coto, a preserve of 67,000 acres, lies between the vast marshy area and the sea. For five centuries it was the hunting preserve of the dukes of Medina-Sidonia, one of whom led the Spanish Armada. The land later passed into the family of Don Mauricio Gonzalez, whose sherry empire stretches around nearby Jerez de la Frontera. In the 1960s much of the area was acquired by the World Wildlife Trust, and the 18-mile trek by horse and mule that was formerly required to reach the Coto was made unnecessary in the very year of our visit by a new automobile road from El Rocio that passes the preserve, and a sandy but passable route that runs from it 6 miles to the sanctuary's headquarters. This headquarters is the Palacio de Doñana; it was once a huge hunting lodge built for a visit by Philip IV of Spain in 1624. Bird finders were welcome to visit the Coto, but we first obtained permission from Dr. Jose A. Alverde, director of the Biological Station of Doñana in Seville.

The Palacio

The Palacio is a fascinating place. It is built around a courtyard, and was designed to accommodate large hunting parties. Rooms and halls are decorated with antlers of stags shot in old hunts, by pictures of hunting parties, and by magnificent photographs of birds taken by Eric Hosking in three expeditions to the Coto in the 1950s. The sandy area around the Palacio is studded with ancient cork oaks, eucalyptus trees, and stone pines, around which grow low plants of which the yellow-flowered halimium is conspicuous. Innumerable semiwild cattle roam the Coto and the Marismas, and the red and fallow deer were amazingly abundant. We were there at the peak of the mating season of the red deer, and were kept awake at night by the roaring of the stags. Once a great wild boar crossed our path, and in the pen outside the Palacio we saw a Spanish wolf and a mongoose, two other types of mammals found in the area. There is a poisonous snake, the Lataste's viper, sinister in appearance with a small horn on its nose. We encountered the driest season in years, and could walk through the parched Marismas, which in rainy months are covered with water.

There was a small staff at the Palacio that kept the rooms and prepared meals with the food we were required to bring with us. In Spanish tradition, dinner was not served until 9:30 P.M., and breakfast twelve hours later. For trips to the distant freshwater lagunas, the sand dunes, and the marshes we could ride horses, but preferred the Land Rover driven by the chief guard.

102 Species at the Coto

Not far from the entrance to the Coto there is an arroyo beside the road that provided us our first impression of the rich birdlife we were to find. Black terns wove back and forth over the water, a water rail skulked along the edge, and a kingfisher dived from its perch. It had brilliant metallic blue-green upper parts and chestnut cheeks and underparts and was only 6^1/$_2$ inches long.

We arrived at the Coto in the late afternoon—having found the gate key in a can in the sand—and on the roof of the Palacio saw numerous starlings. These were the spotless starlings, indistinguishable from our own variety at a distance, but upon closer view found to be without spots.

We were fortunate to meet at the Coto three bird banders, Stuart Pimm and Edward Mackrill, from England, and Heinz Hafner, a Swiss who had just returned from studying the flamingos in the Camargue in France. A few years later, Pimm visited us at Mt. Salem Farm. The three let us see early in the morning the birds they had captured in their mist nets. By the time we arrived in early September they had banded 90 species and some 3,500 individuals, this work being done for the Biological Station of Doñana in Seville. The first great wave of migrants had not arrived by the time of our departure on September 15, and the summer had been severely dry.

The Coto produced several species of hawks and eagles that were entirely new to us. Sometimes they flew high over the parched land, but at other times they were low enough to provide excellent views. Impressive was the Spanish imperial eagle, with blackish brown plumage and yellowish crown and nape. It is now quite rare.

We sighted two smaller eagles, the booted and short-toed. A distinctive species was the buzzard, which in Europe is a dark-brown buteo that hunts from a low altitude by pouncing upon beetles and small animals. Two harriers were added to our list, the marsh and Montagu's. They reminded us of our marsh hawk. A notable species was the red kite; it used to be prevalent in Elizabethan England, but is now extirpated from all Britain except for a few in mountain valleys in Wales. Among the falcons were the kestrels and lesser kestrels, and the hobby, which resembles a small peregrine.

Also of keen interest were the waders we found around two lagunas in the sand dunes and flats. Thirty species of waders, ducks, and other birds enjoyed this habitat. We saw one flock of some 250 flamingos, and, while we were admiring their slender forms and white and rose-pink plumage, another flock of almost the same number flew in. Spoonbills and avocets, ruffs and black-winged stilts added excitement to the scene, as did sandpipers, including the curlew sandpiper. Two grebes, the little and black-necked, swam in the company of several species of ducks, of which the garganey and ferruginous were the most unusual to us. A rare species was the crested coot, similar to our own coot but with a bluish white bill and red knobs on its forehead.

We saw 14 species of warblers, some in the field and some in the banding nets in the morning. On the whole, they were not so brightly colored as our own, but sufficiently attractive. The rufous warbler, for instance, has a long chestnut fantail tipped with black and white. Their names were strange to us: spectacled, melodious, orphean, Cetti's, and Savi's.

Among the other fascinating birds at the Coto were little bustards. These turkeylike birds live in the grassy plains and are very shy. We were fortunate to sight a flock of a score or so flushed by one of the guards on horseback. Another unusual species was the pin-tailed sandgrouse, a pigeonlike groundbird approximately a foot long. A memorable sight was a pair of golden orioles, splendid with bright yellow bodies and black wings and tails.

Birding en Route

After the Coto we drove through Seville, Cadiz, Arcos de la Frontera, Ronda, Granada, Valdepeñas in the Don Quixote country, Toledo, and arrived finally in Madrid. We stopped along the way to see new species, but spent much time watching the people and their ways of life, admiring the scenery, and inspecting notable structures, such as the cathedral in Seville, where we climbed the famed Giralda Tower, and the Alhambra in Granada.

In the marshes outside Cadiz we came upon a flock of a dozen flamingos, a white stork, and an oystercatcher. In Arcos we stood on a high crag and watched a dozen griffon vultures soar over the valley. On the way to Ronda we came upon a group of bee-eaters, amazing birds with chestnut and yellow upper parts, blue-green wings and tails, blue-green under parts, and brilliant yellow throats. We stood on the steep mountain pass at Despen-aperros, "The Pass of the Casting down of the Wild Dogs," and looked down upon the red-rumped swallows threading through the gorge, and in Retiro Park behind the Prado in Madrid we found a score or more of crossbills. This is the same bird as our red crossbill, and the date was September 20.

IRELAND

Our first stop in Ireland was at Leenane, in what has been called "Homeric dream-country." We were accompanied on this trip by Mary and Will Gilman, the same friends who were with us on our trip to Alaska the year before. Leenane is in the Connemara area of County Galway. Our old hotel was at the end of Killary Harbor off the Atlantic. Killary is said to be the loveliest of the Connemara sea loughs or lakes and the only true fiord in Ireland. It is 10 miles long and with a great depth of water that once held a British fleet. Tides rise 18 feet.

Up from the harbor are moors and then mountains that rise steeply 2,000 to 3,000 feet. To the north is Bengorm. To the west is Muilrea ("bald king") and others, and to the east is one called Devil's Mother.

At low tide the edges of the harbor were populated with gulls and beach birds. One was the black-headed gull, a smallish bird with a chocolate-brown head. Another was the common gull, rather like the herring gull; with it were great black-backed and herring gulls. Feeding with the gulls on the beach were four oystercatchers, similar to but not identical with the species found in eastern United States, and a curlew, also slightly different from our own species.

In the vegetation on the moors and up the mountain there were the gray wagtail and the mistle and song thrushes. The mistle thrush is the larger and somewhat reminiscent of our wood thrush, but the song is more melodious. A new species for us was the hooded crow, some 18½ inches long, with gray back and underparts. Ravens were numerous. On one moor we found wrens, similar to our winter wren.

The road from Shannon Airport to Leenane is some 120 miles and passes through Galway and a beautiful if lonely countryside. Along the way we passed vast peat bogs, where the peat was dug by machine to a depth of 10 feet or so and then piled in the shape of bricks or long strips.

Peat is an early stage of decomposition on the way to becoming coal and oil. It dries in two days after being dug. It takes 60 carts of peat to heat a good-sized house for a year. The brown water in the bogs is believed to have certain medicinal qualities, as the turf cutters are said seldom to suffer arthritis or rheumatism. The bog is a preservative, and tubs of butter put there have been found to be fresh after a half century.

Irish Flowers

Ireland is an intensely green land with rich vegetation. We were amazed to find some roads flanked with thick hedges of fuchsia (*Fuchsia magellanica*). This is the familiar bushy shrub with drooping flowers that have crimson calyx, deep purple petals, and very long stamens. It was introduced into Ireland for hedges, and has run wild in some western districts.

When we were walking over a moor, Priscilla discovered an orchis. It had orchid flowers with red spots and a spur. Leaves were linear with dark spots. She determined it was *Orchis elodes*. In the same area she came upon the round-leaved sundew, a carnivorous plant that is common in our New Jersey Pine Barrens.

The Burren

One day when we were still in Leenane we motored down into County Clare to visit the Burren. This botanist's mecca on the west coast of Ireland occupies approximately a seventh of County Clare and a bit of adjoining Galway. It has a coastline of some 25 miles and extends inland for 15. It is a region of pale hills that go up into bold square cliffs and terraces that confront one another over bare and uninhabited plateaus. Its capital is Lisdoonvarna.

The Burren has been described as a "dry skeleton of a country," and one of Cromwell's officers reported it as "a savage place, yielding neither water enough to drown a man, nor wood enough to burn a man, nor soil enough to bury a man." It is a limestone area that was never overwhelmed by glacial drift, peat moor, nor forest, and that is a reason for its unusual plants.

Many are arctic or Alpine species. Showy was the bloody cranesbill, growing lavishly on the rocky slopes and in crevices. Its purplish flowers are solitary, 1 1/2 inches across. Wherever we went we found the dryas or mountain avens, whose blossoms at a distance look like white roses.

The Burren was productive of orchids, plants we found common elsewhere in Ireland. In the Burren there is the early purple orchid, which varies through every shade from deep purple to pure white. One of the rarities is the dense-flowered orchid with minute white, sometimes pinkish flowers. We saw cotton-grass here and elsewhere in Ireland and Iceland, as we had seen it in Alaska. Ferns were plentiful, including the hart's-tongue, which is rare in the United States.

Rosapenna

This spot is in County Donegal, in northwestern Ireland, and from our picnic site one day we could see Malin Head, which is the country's most northern promontory. We were on the Ros-guill Peninsula, which separates Mulroy Bay from Sheep Haven. One of the finest drives in all Ireland is around this peninsula, as the mountainous road looks out to the bays and the Atlantic and over beaches, sheep pastures, and neat houses.

We climbed Melmore Head at the tip of the peninsula, and looked down upon steep cliffs fronting the ocean. The peak was topped by an ancient ruin, a watchtower from which the defenders could sight Vikings and other marauders from the sea. We saw gannets soaring high over the waves. These most spectacular of the breeding seabirds in Ireland nest on three islands to the south, there being some 17,000 nesting pairs on Little Skellig. We did not visit this colony, although we had seen the gannets that nest on Bonaventure Island, off the Gaspé Peninsula in Canada.

Another bird flying over the bases of the cliffs or resting on the water was the black guillemot, a black creature with white patches on its wings. A long, rocky promontory extended from the cliffs, and this was used as a resting place for a dozen oyster-catchers. Gulls and cormorants flew by constantly.

On the way to Melmore Head and along the drive of some 180 miles from Leenane to Rosapenna we enjoyed many of Ireland's land birds. Noteworthy was the wheatear, the size of a sparrow and with blue-gray back, white rump, and white sides to the tail. In Ireland the rectangular fields are separated by magnificent gray stone fences, often as high as a man's shoulders. Fields and fences are favorite spots for wheatears and meadow pipits, the latter very similar to our own water pipits.

The last bird I shall mention is the noble bullfinch, which we saw first on a fence near Yeats' burial place outside Sligo. It is a striking bird, with bright rose-red under parts, blue-gray upper parts, black cap and chin, and very heavy black bill.

We saw only seven species in Ireland that were new to us, chiefly because we had enjoyed two previous trips to England, where the birds are very similar. Birding in Ireland is comforting and rewarding, but not very exciting.

ICELAND

Our first day in Iceland was when we landed in Reykjavik in mid-July. We viewed through the wind and rain the country's rather desolate countryside, a monotony relieved by mountains, large lakes, and such natural phenomena as waterfalls, geysers, and hot springs. The only birds of note that we saw that day were an arctic skua (our parasitic jaeger), many whimbrels, and redshanks.

Shortly after leaving Reykjavik we crossed a lava field and then to Thingvallavatn, Iceland's largest lake, and to Thingvellir, a dramatic plain of black lava, much of it covered with moss. This is the ancient site of Iceland's Althing, said to be the oldest legislative body in the world still in existence.

We next visited Great Geysir, from which our name "geyser" is derived. It is now rather lazy, but another geyser performed for us. In the area were numerous hot springs, some emitting large clouds of steam. Our last sight this day was the Gullfoss (Golden Falls), claimed to be one of the most notable waterfalls in Europe. The water thunders down double falls into a deep gorge.

Better Birding

Our next day provided better birding. We drove southeast from Reykjavik and around the Reykjanes Peninsula. It is an area of rough lava fields that end at the ocean in steep cliffs. We found one large rock in the ocean that was covered with hundreds of fulmars. Puffins darted in and out of large crevices in the cliffs. Eiders swam in the offshore waters, and a large flock of kittiwakes streamed by.

Inland from the sea but still in the area of lava rocks and volcanic grit we almost ran down a baby golden plover. We photographed it, admiring its golden plumage, while the distraught parents performed the typical plover broken-wing act to distract our attention. There were many golden plovers in grassy areas around small bodies of water, sometimes flying in small compact flocks.

Another find was the great skua, of which we saw many. This hawklike seabird is approximately the size of a herring gull, but much stockier in body and with uniformly dark plumage. It is related to the arctic skua, which was much more numerous. We saw also a pomarine skua. The skuas seen off the United States are called jaegers. On this trip we sighted also Iceland and glaucous gulls.

Fire and Ice

Iceland has been called the "Land of Fire and Ice." It is one of the most volcanic regions of the earth, with 107 volcanoes and thousands of vents. Mt. Hekla erupted in May 1970. When we flew from Glasgow to Reykjavik we passed over a large new island named Surtsey, which was created out of the sea by a volcanic eruption in 1963. Roughly a tenth of the total area of Iceland is postglacial lava. Our lunar astronauts went to Iceland to study the lava before their moon trips.

Approximately 13 percent of Iceland is covered by snow-fields and 120 glaciers. The largest is Vatnajökull, which is also the largest glacier in Europe. Yet, Icelanders lament that they do not have enough snow suitable for skiing.

The geysers and hot springs are caused by the same source as active volcanoes. The water in the springs comes out at 275 degrees Fahrenheit, and is conducted through large insulated pipes to heat residential and commercial buildings. We visited a large series of greenhouses heated this way, and saw trees bearing bananas, big bunches of grapes on the vines, and luxuriant tomatoes.

The climate is said to lack extremes because the island is washed by a branch of the Gulf Stream, providing an average temperature only one degree lower than in New York. Only the northern tip of Iceland is within the Arctic Circle.

Akureyri

Akureyri is a town of some 10,000 population, the second largest in Iceland. It is less than 50 miles from the Arctic Circle, and as the north wind had been blowing, I wore Icelandic mittens. It is a picturesque place, situated at the head of the largest fiord in Iceland and surrounded by mountains. The manners of its people are rather rough, and in the streets below us at night we saw residents throwing bottles at one another and heard the crash of glass.

For such a small community, Akureyri is unusually progressive in some ways. We visited its natural history museum and saw specimens of the 76 species of birds that have been found in Iceland. We also walked in the botanical gardens, and saw examples of the many wild and garden flowers that grow in the country. The gardens were thronged with redpolls that ate seeds or drank from the pools that sustained water plants. The harbor below teemed with hundreds of arctic terns and eiders, the latter appearing in family groups. Along the streets we found the redwing (a thrush) and the pied wagtail.

One reason for the small number of birds in Iceland is that the country is practically treeless except for the Akureyri area. The land was covered with trees from the ocean to the mountains when the settlers came, but they denuded it. Since there are no trees there are no woodpeckers and only a dozen perching birds. The trees in Akureyri are small willows and birches. Many of the buildings in Iceland must be built of iron because of lack of wood.

Lake Myvatn

One time we rode 60 miles east of Akureyri to Lake Myvatn. This is the third largest lake in Iceland, and is noted for its breeding ducks. When we were in Reykjavik we visited Dr. Finnur Gudmundsson, director of the natural history museum there, who said that some 20,000 ducks of 13 species were then breeding at Myvatn. None of the ducks was new to us, as many were the same as our own species and others have appeared occasionally in our area, such as the tufted duck, Barrow's goldeneye, and harlequin.

Myvatn is Icelandic for "Fly Lake," because of the enormous clouds of black flies. We encountered none in late July. The lake is fed by mineral springs that encourage vegetation in its shallow waters. This food and the black-fly larvae are relished by breeding waterfowl. The midges are also the prey of tasty trout that provided our luncheon at the lake.

On the eastern side of the lake we walked through Black Castles—rocks, caves, and canyons formed by flowing lava some 2,000 years ago. Near the lake are two pools of natural hot mineral water in underground caves. Men use one pool for bathing in the nude, women the other pool. Sulphur pits and hot springs abound.

Mt. Hekla

To reach Mt. Hekla you take a picturesque route through the valley of the Thjorsa, the longest river in Iceland. Hekla is an active volcano, and in former times was considered unmistakable evidence of the existence of hell. There was an eruption in 1947 that lasted a year, and on May 5, 1970, there was another eruption from 20 craters, and the lava, pumice, and ash covered an area of some 25 square miles. An estimated 200 million cubic yards of lava were erupted. We went to the edge of the new lava, which presented a wall 60 to 100 feet high. It was not a solid mass, but broken into huge chunks that were still warm, heat waves rising from some areas. In one place the lava was still moving, showing red. Not far from Hekla we came upon a beautiful glen in this area of volcanic desolation. It was deep, fed by two waterfalls, and rich in grass and buttercups.

BIRDS OF THE OCEAN

Once when we took a ship to England, the gray Atlantic which we crossed at the rate of approximately 460 miles a day introduced us to several species of seabirds. One was the fulmar, which is related to the petrels and shearwaters. It is some 18 inches long, and looks somewhat like a herring gull, but has a bull neck and stubby body. These birds followed the ship in mid-ocean, gliding and banking close to the waves in the manner of shearwaters. The fulmar is strictly a seabird, breeding colonially on oceanic cliffs and islands, as we saw them doing later in Iceland. We found the bird at 50 degrees north latitude, a line that runs from Labrador to southern England.

We saw three kinds of shearwaters, the sooty, Cory's, and greater. The first two species appeared mainly over the waters off Cape Cod and Nova Scotia; thereafter we found only the greater shearwater. The shearwaters are between 16 and 18 inches long, and bank and glide on long, narrow, stiff wings. When the white underparts of the greater shearwater are exposed in the sunlight, the birds are very conspicuous, but when they wheel their dark brown upper parts make them almost invisible against the waves.

Most exciting bird was the long-tailed skua, which in America is known as the long-tailed jaeger. One day when we were approximately 1,200 miles at sea, four of these handsome birds flew close over the open aft deck. We could view plainly their two very long and flexible center tail feathers, their black caps and white underparts.

We saw also the arctic skua, known in America as the parasitic jaeger. It was harassing the kittiwakes, a species of gulls that at 16 inches is 2 inches smaller than its oppressor. The arctic skuas we sighted were in juvenal plumage, darkish brown creatures that were hawklike in both appearance and flight. This piratical species breeds on the bleak moors and tundras of the Arctic.

St. Peter's Birds

We added to our list the Leach's and storm petrels, small blackish birds with white rumps that flit over the waves much in the manner of swallows. Sometimes petrels dangle their feet and appear to be walking on the water, thus duplicating the perform-ance of St. Peter and providing the reason for their name. We saw the Leach's petrels on the first part of the voyage, and were able to distinguish at short range the distinct brownish cast of their plumage. When we were halfway across the Atlantic the storm petrels began to appear over the wake of our ship. They are darker and smaller than the Leach's, and habitually follow ships well out from land, a characteristic which the Leach's petrel lacks.

The petrels, shearwaters, and fulmars visit land only to breed. They rest on the water, and we passed many small flocks of shearwaters that were riding the waves. When we came within sight of the English coast we lost all these birds and saw only great black-backed and herring gulls and gannets.

My wife and I were the only two birders among the 1,200 passengers on the S. S. *Hanseatic*. However, we interested some other passengers who also had binoculars, and we formed a short-lived Hanseatic Bird Club.

Gaspé Peninsula

After driving a thousand miles from Caldwell in New Jersey, on a route that passed through Quebec and followed the St. Lawrence River, we reached Cap Bon Ami. It is a magnificent look-out spot, one of the three extreme tips of the Gaspé Peninsula. Here the mountains meet the Gulf of St. Lawrence, in some places abruptly, in others separated from the water by broad and pleasant meadows where tiny French villages are situated. The name Gaspé is from the Indian, meaning "the end," and the word is well illustrated by Bon Ami.

As we stood on the heights overlooking the gulf, we saw broad waters where gannets, cormorants, guillemots, and gulls were feeding. Above us, along the mountain ridge, we heard the croaking of ravens, and saw these somber birds coasting over the treetops. The spruces and hardwoods around our camp were thronged with warblers, chiefly myrtles (now called yellow-rumped warbler) but accompanied by redstarts, magnolia, and black-throated green warblers. Everywhere we heard the thin notes of kinglets.

Here we met by arrangement Dr. and Mrs. Adrian Sabety of Montclair, who had departed three weeks previously. He is a thoracic surgeon. While fishing along the Cascapedia River, Dr. Sabety had been startled to see a gray-cheeked thrush alight on his fishing pole, and had then looked up to sight a great antlered moose across the stream. They had seen flocks of evening grosbeaks and some boreal chickadees, and had listed a black-backed woodpecker and an olive-sided flycatcher.

After we left Quebec, the road soared, dipped, and followed the edge of the St. Lawrence, passing through Ste. Jean-Port-Joli, Rivière-du-Loup, Trois-Pistoles, Cap-Chat, Rivière-aux-Renauds, and many another pleasant village. In each, the church was the most conspicuous structure, attesting the deeply religious nature of this people. Back from the river ran the Shickshock Mountains, the tip of the Appalachian chain; they are substantial peaks, with an average height of 3,300 feet. We saw our first gannets along the river and also a string of common eiders, some whimbrels, turnstones, and great blue herons.

We spent three days tenting in Gaspesian National Park. You turn off the road at Ste. Anne-des-Monts to enter this 2,500-square-mile tract of the High Shickshocks. The tenting area is 20 miles into the forest, at the foot of Mt. Albert. Along this way we saw the sad devastation of a forest fire that had burned for two weeks in July, destroying 150 square miles of timber. The woods were still smoldering.

The park contains many streams and lakes, and these attract birds. At Lake Coté we found red crossbills and ruffed grouse, and along the stream where we camped the pine grosbeaks fed in the conifers. Gray Jays and juncos came to our camp table for tidbits. The woods in early morning were alive with warblers.

There was a flock of Nashville warblers, a few Blackburnians, and also chestnut-sided, black-throated green, magnolia, and many myrtle warblers. Pine siskins and cedar waxwings were abundant.

The dominant flower everywhere on the peninsula is the fireweed, as it seems to be in Alaska and Iceland. The Canada thistle, Canada goldenrod, and pearly everlasting also made conspicuous displays. On the floor of the forest the bunchberry showed its clusters of red berries, and the *Clintonia borealis* held erect its spikes of blue fruit.

It was cold up in the north woods, and one night it was so bitter we had to crawl out of our sleeping bags at 3 A.M. to build a fire and drink hot coffee. It was around 30 degrees in Quebec, we heard, and it had been raining, so the ground was damp beneath us. The air went out of my mattress, and I awakened shivering from sleeping on the cold, wet ground. While the coffee was brewing, we had a bottle of prepared martinis from which we imbibed at this unusual hour. It was a rewarding experience, however, for the sky was bright with the greenish blue banners of the northern lights.

From Cap Bon Ami we drove to Percé and Bonaventure Island. As we approached the village of Percé from Mt. Ste. Anne, we looked down upon the loveliest view of our trip along the Gaspé Peninsula. We saw the little houses with their red and blue roofs, a giant cross that had been erected on a lonely hill, then, offshore, the massive monolith that is Percé Rock and, farther away, Bonaventure Island.

We made two boat trips around Bonaventure Island to see the great colonies of gannets that nested on its eastern cliffs. As the boat left the shore we passed Percé Rock, so named because it is pierced by a large opening at water level, and we noted the typical great cormorants and herring gulls that nested on its seemingly unscalable top. When we rounded the island we were amazed to see the thousands of gannets massed on the ledges facing the gulf. Approximately 20,000 birds nested there, whitening the cliffs as they crowded one another for space on the narrow shelves. This colony of gannets is the fourth largest of the 22 known to exist in North America and Europe. At one time this colony was almost extirpated by fishermen, who killed them with clubs and cut them up for bait.

On one of the ledges we sighted four black-and-white, erect birds that stood in the shadow of a ponderous boulder, almost as if hiding. These were the creatures we most wanted to see on this trip, the curious puffins. We asked the captain to retrace his route so we could get a better look, and on the return passage found yet another bird. The puffin is sometimes called *sea parrot* because of its great beak, which is banded red, blue, and yellow, and appears only in breeding season. The bird is more than a foot long with black back, collar and crown, and white face and underparts. It stands and walks erect. After the breeding season it goes to sea, so we were fortunate to find it. In winter the puffin appears casually as far south as New Jersey. This is the common puffin, the only one that appears in the North Atlantic. Later, when we visited Alaska, we found the similar horned puffin and the tufted puffin.

Black guillemots or sea pigeons were common around the island, displaying large white patches on their wings as they flew. A flock of kittiwakes brightened the waters near the gannet colony, and there were numerous black-backed gulls. Earlier in the season murres and razorbills breed on Bonaventure, but they had returned to their nomadic life at sea by the time of our arrival.

On our second trip around the island we landed and climbed to the crest of the cliffs. There we were able to approach within four or five feet of the hundreds of gannets that had chosen that area rather than the face of the cliffs as their nesting place. We took almost a hundred photographs at this close range. The gannet is 3 feet long and has a wingspread of 4. There were many young birds in various plumages, and all were making a loud din.

Driving along the south shore of the peninsula and the northern edge of Chaleur Bay, we came to the Petite Cascapedia

River, where we spent one day. We wished we could have remained longer, as there were evening and pine grosbeaks feeding in the conifers, warblers passing in migration, and brown creepers and red-breasted nuthatches exploring the tree trunks.

On our way home we felt impelled to visit Biddeford Pool, one of the best spots for shorebirds in Maine. It is at the town of Biddeford, just south of Portland, and is a tidal bay sheltered by dunes and ledges. The mud flats, which were exposed at low tide, had attracted hundreds of black-bellied plovers, and ringed plovers were also abundant. We found three of the terns—common, arctic, and roseate; and three gulls—the Bonaparte's, laughing, and herring.

7

BUGS
AND BEASTS

The most fearsome bug on Mt. Salem Farm is the tick. It is an arachnid allied with spiders, rather than an insect. One day a lovely lady who was our guest was bitten by an infected tick at our place and developed Rocky Mountain spotted fever. This is a severe malady, characterized at its onset by chills, fever, severe headache, and pains in joints and bones. A rash usually appears about the fifth or sixth day and is a mottled red color, scattered first over wrists and ankles. Later the rash becomes darker and covers the abdomen and back. She recovered after several months of illness. When my family went West we had injections of the vaccine, and now take them annually. There is not much Rocky Mountain spotted fever in New Jersey, and not all ticks are infected. Before present-day medicine, mortality was high.

I have read in a dispatch from New England that ticks are attracted by exhaust from automobiles, hence may become more numerous along roadsides. An aracologist (expert on ticks, mites, and relatives) in Waltham, Massachusetts, discovered this in studies of tick distribution in Massachusetts. He believes that today's volume of carbon dioxide produced by motor cars is responsible.

He says: "The fact that carbon dioxide lures ticks has long been known by aracologists. A common device is a small block of dry ice which becomes carbon dioxide as it evaporates. If dry ice is placed in a field, ticks will migrate toward it."

I found ticks very numerous in Massachusetts when we used to spend vacations on Cape Cod. Once I walked in a field there and found the ticks infesting the tops of the grasses, with the result that the bottoms of my trousers were literally covered with them.

Daddy Longlegs

One morning we saw an interesting design on the screen that covers the large glass doors to the kitchen. It was made by two groups each of five daddy longlegs and the creatures in each group had arranged themselves in a circle. Since the distance between the opposite legs of this relative of the spiders is at least five inches, they made an unusual display.

The daddy longlegs is not an insect, but is in the class of Arachnida, which includes the spiders, ticks, chiggers, and scorpions. It is harmless and has several common names, including grandfather graybeard. It is also called harvestman, and the French call it haymaker, as the creatures appear in greater number at the time of haymaking. Since the farmer across the road from our farm had just finished baling his hay, the last name seems especially appropriate.

The body of the daddy longlegs is a small oval, hardly bigger than a large grain of wheat. There are four pairs of long, slender legs, each seven-jointed. One pair, the longest, is used to explore the surroundings. These two legs are kept in rapid motion, their tips transmitting useful intelligence.

A pastime of country children is to demand the daddy longlegs to point out where the family's cows have strayed. This is done by grasping one of the long legs and watching the direction in which most of the others point. Fortunately, the creature has the power to grow new legs to replace those lost.

The longlegs feed upon small insects, decaying vegetable matter, and plant juices. I saw one nibbling a small moth. Another creature that is called daddy longlegs is an insect, the crane fly. It may be more than two inches long, and is sometimes mistaken for a large mosquito, but it does not bite.

Chiggers

I have been bitten by chiggers in Florida, North Carolina, and Virginia, where these troublesome mites thrive, so I believe I know a chigger bite when I feel it. I haven't had many chigger bites here at the farm, but they are annoying.

The chigger is a red, undeveloped form of mite, distantly related to the spiders. It apparently must become a parasite in order to live, so attaches itself to some domesticated animal, bird, or human being. A person walking through deep grass is likely to come in contact with one of these creatures. When in crawling over the skin it meets an obstacle, such as a belt, it is likely to stop and bite, fastening itself to the surface of the skin. In biting the chigger injects into the epidermis a squirt of saliva which helps it digest the victim's skin. It is the saliva that makes one itch. After a few hours of feeding externally, the male chigger gets all the food it needs and drops off, but the victim itches worse after it is gone than while it is still grazing. The female burrows into the skin, causing an ulcer through which the eggs are released.

According to one authority, the itching can be relieved by touching the area with rubbing alcohol three times a day, followed immediately with some anti-itching oil, such as boric-acid ointment to which a little phenol has been added. Another remedy is to use nail polish. A friend told us that once, on a field trip, the only polish available was a bright red. When she had dabbed her bites with this, she appeared to be afflicted with a serious disease.

Periodical Cicada

The year 1970 saw the emergence in our area of Brood X of the seventeen-year cicada. These insects are erroneously called locusts, but the name *locust* is applied correctly only to certain species of grasshoppers.

In our region the periodical cicada comes out every seventeen years, but in the South the period is thirteen years. After years of living in underground tunnels, millions of the insects emerge as if on signal, undergo amazing transformations, spread through trees and bushes, and fill the air with their droning songs. After mating and laying the eggs they die. This cicada is widely distributed over the eastern half of the United States, but occurs nowhere else in the world.

The adult is approximately 1½ inches long, with black body, reddish legs, nearly transparent wings and red eyes. It does not feed on foliage and does not sting. The female uses a sawlike egg-laying apparatus at the end of the abdomen to puncture twigs and make little pockets in the wood. In each pocket she lays some two dozen eggs and continues this process until approximately 500 eggs are laid.

The eggs are hatched in six or seven weeks, and the immature insects are called nymphs. The nymphs fall to the ground and burrow 18 to 24 inches below until they find suitable roots from which to suck juices. This is the beginning of their seventeen years underground.

In these years the nymphs become fully grown and start burrowing upward, and toward the end of May in northern areas they come out of the ground in vast numbers, leaving holes the diameter of one's small finger, and head for the bushes and trees. They secure a good hold, and in a few hours appear as fully adult cicadas. The adults mate within a week, the female lays eggs within a few days, and the adults then die within five or six weeks.

The fact that periodical cicadas in the North have a seventeen-year cycle does not mean that they are seen only at seventeen-year intervals. They appear somewhere almost every year because there are different broods that emerge in different years. Those that come out within any given year comprise a brood, those that emerge the next year comprise a different brood, and so on. Most of the broods are separated geographically, but some overlap.

The broods have been designated by Roman numerals. The numerals I through XVII are assigned to the seventeen-year broods, another series to the thirteen-year broods. This numeration began with the 1893 brood, which was designated Brood I. Brood X, the largest to occur over much of the northeastern United States, appeared in 1936, 1953, and 1970.

The songs of the three species of seventeen-year cicadas vary from toadlike trills through various ticks and buzzes. The volume of sound is amazing, literally filling the air. In 1970 we drove to Washington and back, and along the way seemed to be passing through a wall of sound. A friend told me that the noise was so great in Princeton that it shut out the roar of traffic in the center of the borough.

I noticed considerable damage done to deciduous trees by the females that punctured the twigs to make holes to deposit eggs. The twigs tended to break off at the puncture, and large masses of dead leaves could be seen amidst the foliage.

We took two of the nymphs home and put them in a drinking glass. In the morning they had split their skins and the adult insects were clinging to the twigs we had put in the glass with them. The birds relished cicadas, and we saw them being eaten by grackles and being fed by adult bluebirds to their young in a nest we were photographing.

Troublesome Insects

Two troublesome insects are the sweat bee (genus *Halictus*) and pine sawfly. The sweat bee is so-called because it is fond of alighting upon perspiring persons. I was swinging a scythe on a hot day in June and perspiring profusely. Since both my hands were occupied, I was defenseless against bees that stung me on each temple. The effect was startling. My face puffed up like a balloon and both eyes were practically closed. With the aid of an injection and oral doses of cortisone, I came back to normal in three days. A physician friend later gave me a bee kit, which included a hypodermic syringe with an adrenalin-type substance and antihistamine pills.

I have been bitten by these bees in the past, and perhaps that was my trouble. When the allergic reaction is severe, it is believed the victim has developed a sensitivity from previous exposure. However, persons who are allergic to bee stings may develop an immunity by repeated injections of the bee venom, although this is dangerous. As a boy I appeared to have developed an immunity to mosquito stings, a different irritation, because I lived in Rutherford on the edge of the Hackensack Meadows before the mosquito-extermination commissions had performed their effective work.

The pine sawfly is a pest imported from Europe. It feeds on our Austrian pines, although it does not seem to bother the white pines. The larvae are an inch long, with black heads and greenish yellow bodies. They live in colonies on the ends of branches of the pines, gradually consuming the needles. They assume peculiar positions, sometimes lying supine, at other times with the end of the abdomen curled and held aloft. If disturbed, the whole colony will move at once from one position to the other.

Mud Dauber

Driving to Clinton one early July day I noticed a clay tube more than an inch long attached to the speedometer. I recognized this as the nest of a mud dauber, one of the 70 species of mud wasps that are found in our country. Upon returning home I broke off the capsule carefully, being curious as to its contents. Inside were a tiny grub, the larva of the wasp, and 10 small spiders of 3 species. The spiders were not dead, but they moved only feebly. They were the food supply that the grub would consume as it matured.

The story of the mud dauber is curious. The wasp is a slender black creature whose body gives off glints of steel and blue. In early summer the female seeks mud from the edges of ponds and puddles, mixing it with saliva from her mouth to make a firm cement. She plasters the cement in some protected place, making a tube approximately an inch long, with walls an eighth of an inch thick. She does the plastering with her jaws, using them as a trowel. When the tube is completed save for an open end, she collects spiders. These are the meat upon which the wasp's grub will feed. They must be kept fresh for two or three weeks, so the wasp thrusts her sting into the spider's nervous system in such a way that the victim is not killed but paralyzed and made defenseless against the growing grub. After the mud dauber has stored the cell with spiders, she lays an egg within it, makes more cement, and closes the open end of the tube.

Inside the mud cell the wasp larva grows until all the spider meat is consumed. It then weaves about itself a cocoon which covers the inside of the mud home. Within the cocoon it changes into a pupa, and when it emerges finally it is a full-grown wasp, whose jaws are strong enough to cut open the end of the tube so that it can get out.

The automobile stood in the garage unused only a day and two nights, so one must marvel at the mud dauber's industry.

Creatures of the Night

Lights on our patio have attracted night-flying creatures, especially moths. One night they lured two species of giant silk moths, polyphemus and luna. Although the luna moth is called the most beautiful North American insect, we were more impressed by the larger polyphemus. It is named after the one-eyed chief of the Cyclops, who imprisoned Odysseus and his companions in a cave. Our two specimens have a wingspread of 5 inches, the ochre hind wings each displaying a large transparent eyespot, bordered by blue and set in a black ring. The antennae are feathery, three-quarters of an inch long.

The polyphemus is one of our native silk moths, as are the luna, cecropia, and promethea. Its caterpillar is a beautiful shade of green, ornamented on the sides by lines of silvery white. The cocoons are attached to oaks, maples, and birches, and drop to the ground in the fall. The cocoon is dense, and contains a long, unbroken thread of silk.

The luna moth was smaller, measuring four inches across its wings, its light green freed from uniformity by eyespots that are bordered by rings of yellow, blue, and black. The wings have margins of purple and yellow, and the hind wings are extended in long tails.

The luna moth has been called "Empress of the Night." It is named after the Roman goddess of the moon and of months. Its long swallow tails give it a graceful shape, and may afford it some protection. During the day it hangs with wings down beneath the green leaves, and the folded projections of the hind wings resemble a leaf stem, making the insect appear to be a large leaf.

Another night we were visited by three quite different moths, the rosy maple moth, the blinded sphinx, and the io moth. The rosy maple moth is a beautiful insect with a wingspread of approximately 2 inches, the wings being a fluffy combination of rose and pale yellow. Its larvae feed upon maples, and it is most abundant in the Middle West. The blinded sphinx moth also has a wingspread of some 2 inches, the forewings being brown and rather angular, and the hind wings marked by a silvery blue eyespot, set in a black ring and surrounded by an area of yellow. The larva feeds chiefly upon plants of the rose family. Most spectacular of the three insects was the io moth (*Automeris io*), named after Io, a Greek moon goddess. It is larger than the other two moths, its wings being generally yellow and reddish, the hind wings each containing a large black eyespot with a silver center. These eyespots on the wings of polyphemus and other species of moths are believed to be protective devices that might frighten predators, or at least give them pause. The caterpillar of the io is almost omnivorous. It must be handled with care, as its spines have severe stinging properties.

Declining Populations

Everyone comments upon the smaller populations of moths and butterflies. A neighbor who has long made a hobby of moths says he has not seen a promethea moth for years, yet when I was a boy in New Jersey they were relatively common. There has been some speculation that these declining insect populations, which have been observed elsewhere in the United States and abroad, have been caused by pesticides, radioactive fallout, and man-made radio interference with the insects' mating signals. The prevalent opinion, however, is that the decline has been caused by the bulldozer, not the spray gun. Urbanization has destroyed much of the natural habitat of the insects. Some, such as cabbage butterflies, thrive on crops raised in new environments. I can attest to the abundance of the little white cabbage butterflies, as their green larvae are giving me a stern battle for possession of my broccoli.

The German Society for the Protection of Alpine Flowers and Animals says that nature watchers who could formerly "routinely rejoice in counting 500 to 600 butterflies of some 50 genera in a warm and sunny hour in the afternoon . . . today can barely reach up to 40 butterflies of a dozen genera." In London the wife of a British Cabinet minister even proposed that the city breed butterflies to brighten its parks.

Breeding Moths

I have been puzzled by the lack since our first year here of silk moths at our farm, but our neighbors, Laura and Bill Riley, have had some interesting experiences. One day Laura received some cocoons of the promethea moth from a friend in Illinois whose hobby is rearing moths. A week later the moths emerged from the cocoons and proved to be three females. Laura kept the insects in a box Bill had contrived that was covered with wire netting. Much to her surprise next morning she found three other and darker moths clinging to the outside of the cage. After studying the books and conferring with Joseph Muller of Lebanon, the authority in our area on moths and butterflies, we determined these new arrivals were male tulip-tree moths (*Callosamia angulifera*). They obviously had been attracted by the three females of *Callosamia promethea*. Incidentally, the tulip tree, also called the tulip tree poplar, is prominent in our locality.

What strange sense brought these male tulip-tree moths out of distant trees to find the female prometheas? Neither the Rileys nor I have ever seen a tulip-tree moth. Mr. Muller says that sometimes the two species interbreed and that the tulip-tree moth is not so unusual as supposed.

One theory is that a scent given off by the female is the attraction. Henri Fabre experimented with peacock moths, and assumed that the males could detect the female scent (which our human nostrils cannot detect at an inch) from a distance of nearly a mile. The males have large and feathery antennae clothed with sensitive bristles and hairs of various kinds. Those of the females are of comparatively simple structure. Some writers believe that these complex feathery feelers enable the male moths to scent from afar the objects of their affection.

Fabre found also that materials against which female moths had rested would for some time afterward attract the male moths, which seemed further proof that smell was the agent of attraction. However he tried to mask this subtle smell with naphthaline, sulphureted hydrogen, oil of lavender, paraffin, and other agents.

Still the male moths continued to come, so Fabre began to doubt that the attraction was smell. He asked, "But what is materially emitted? Nothing, according to our sense of smell. And this nothing is supposed to saturate an immense circle several miles in radius with its molecules? However divisible this matter may be, the mind refuses to accept such conclusions."

Another theory that Fabre approached tentatively was that females broadcast for a mate, setting in motion waves capable of spreading to distances incompatible with a real diffusion of matter.

John J. Ward in his later *Mystery Senses of Insects* suggests the theory of wave emanation may be a solution to the phenomenon. "Even the fact of the male moths visiting objects upon which the female moths have rested (one of the chief planks of the scent theory) is then no longer a puzzle, for it is the property of rays to penetrate, and often to leave a record behind." He concludes that the moth's sensory feelers may be organs specialized for receiving delicate radio vibrations, probably of the nature of infrared or heat rays, which in the wave spectrum come just below those of visible light.

Laura is having an interesting time rearing moths. She was concerned with three of the silk moths, the polyphemus, promethea, and luna, and with two other species, the sphinx and io.

Bill's boxes with screen facings house large bottles in which the moths are kept in their various stages of development. The prometheas had for the most part made cocoons by the end of August, but the others had not, and so were fed fresh leaves of the trees they prefer. These trees include ash, walnut, maple, and spicebush. The luna caterpillars have enormous appetites, and they are so numerous that they consume each day leaves of between 30 and 40 small branches of the walnut. In feeding, it was necessary to be extremely careful lest the tiny larvae be crushed by the hand or against the side of a jar.

Laura is interested in increasing the population of the attractive moths and in studying their life cycles.

Banding Butterflies

You hear much about banding birds, but who bands butterflies? One of my readers, Mrs. Helen Raub of Chatham, does. She is cooperating with the University of Toronto in a project to discover the migration patterns of the monarch butterfly and the disease that kills it. Some 400 other persons are participating. Each receives small metal tags to be fastened to one of the insect's wings, and everyone is requested to send to the university the wing of any dead monarch to which the Toronto tag is affixed.

Mrs. Raub grows milkweed on her property, as it is the favorite food plant of the monarch, and from these and other sources she collects eggs. In late August one year she had some 200 caterpillars, 50 of them ready for the chrysalis stage. She hoped to obtain at least 100 monarch butterflies to band. She photographed the life cycle of the butterfly from caterpillar and cocoon through the emergence of the adult insect.

Froghopper

The other day I was in a field where the stems of young goldenrod plants were covered with a white, frothy substance that aroused my curiosity. I probed into some with a knife blade, and found that each mass of froth sheltered a few nymphs, or an immature form of an insect called the froghopper. The nymphs were pale yellow, although the mature froghoppers are usually brown. The insect is small and squat, and has a froggy appearance as it rests on a plant.

This foamy substance is the castle of the froghopper; it spends its early days in this bubbly mass, sheltered from the direct sun and kept moist by the foam. The castle also protects it from enemies.

The frothy substance is composed of excess sap which the froghopper has sucked from the plant and into which it has blown bubbles. The insect has overlapping plates beneath its abdomen which form a kind of bicycle pump, into which air is drawn and expelled. It blows this air into the sap to produce the froth. This substance is sometimes called cuckoo spit, and the froghoppers are called spittle bugs.

The nymphs of the froghoppers are not the only creatures living in the foam castles. The larvae of a fly, one of the tiny vinegar or fruit flies, also live in the froth as harmless guests of the froghopper nymphs.

Dance of the Mayflies

At dinner one evening we looked out on the aerial dance of the Mayflies. Large hatches of these insects came out on several evenings, and in their mating flights they executed a fluttering ascent and descent, the process repeated continually.

The Mayfly was formerly classified as the family Ephemeridae, from the Greek meaning lasting a day. The life of the adult may extend only one or two days, the insects taking no food during their fugitive existences. The span from egg to adult insect may last three years, however.

There are 470 species. Our variety has delicately formed bodies, segmented antennae, one pair of net-veined membranous wings, and two long threadlike caudal filaments. The larvae or nymphs frequent sandy bottoms of streams, hide beneath stones, or attach themselves to water plants. Eventually the nymphs swim to the surface of the water and a fissure appears in their backs, from which the winged insects emerge and fly away in a few seconds.

Sometimes the appearance of adult Mayflies is in such great numbers as to inconvenience passersby. I have seen such hordes of the creatures on the shores of Lake Michigan that they coated the highways with their slippery substance and impeded traffic.

Mayflies are relished by trout, and a favorite dryfly of the fishermen, the "gray drake," is made in imitation of them.

Fireflies

Observations on fireflies are offered by Robert May, Jr., of West Caldwell, a longtime correspondent. He lives on the edge of Hatfield Swamp, and has found six species of fireflies there, not counting three that are not luminous. The best display is made by *Photuris pennsylvanica,* a variety that prefers open fields. The first of these appear in late May, and they persist until mid-August. They reach their peak of activity in early July, and in the meadow where bird watchers were wont to watch bobolinks, thousands of field fireflies were flashing their signals, at the rate of approximately two flashes a second. At close range the light is greenish. Mr. May says they start their display toward the end of evening when the lawn fireflies are putting out their lights, and keep on flashing till long after midnight.

Another species of firefly occurs only in the open grassy fields of Hatfield Swamp, and this is an early variety, disappearing by the middle of June. A species of *Photinus* frequents the wet meadows and flashes a yellowish light among the sedges and docks. The female can fly. but rarely does so. She sits in the grass instead, languidly flashing her signals. If a male is nearby he answers with a flash of his own and flies toward her. Another species of *Photinus* is the largest firefly of all. Mr. May calls this the great firefly; he has given his own names to others also, as the swamp firefly, lawn firefly, and wet meadow firefly.

Crickets

In walking through the woods we find it rewarding to lift old logs and flat stones and tear off the bark of dead trees. We discover salamanders under the logs and stones and cave crickets beneath the bark of trees. We were engaged in this pursuit near a wooded pond in Sussex County and found only one salamander, the long-tailed, a rather nondescript creature, but did uncover a cluster of seven or eight cave crickets.

These crickets have to be seen to be believed, because they are so big. The body is almost an inch long, and the insect stretches 4 inches from tips of forelegs to hindlegs. The feelers alone are 3 inches long. The creatures are narrow-bodied and hump-backed, and are sometimes called camel crickets. They live in caves or other moist places, and the spot where we found them was next to some cliffs that had deep and dark recesses.

We found another fascinating cricket in the Pine Barrens, the mole cricket. It is so-called because of habits and structure that are similar to those of the Eastern mole. We noticed a burrow in the bog sand and, digging down, unearthed the cricket. Its body is thick and cylindrical and covered with short, fine hairs that give it a furry appearance. The body is an inch and a quarter long, but its legs and antennae are much shorter than those of the cave cricket. It tunnels by using its front legs, which are short and flattened, somewhat resembling a hand. The mole cricket feeds upon other insects and even upon the weaker members of its own species.

White-faced Hornet

Recently I extended my grape arbor, and shortly thereafter found rather large hornets chewing the new wood. They were black with white markings, and their tearing into the wood was energetic and audible. I knew they were getting pulp for their paper nest, and found the structure, large, globular, and gray, hanging some 10 feet above ground in a spruce tree. We have seen these nests with a definite reddish hue, the result of the insects having chewed for their purpose the red No Hunting signs posted on trees.

Later the nest appeared abandoned, although the insects were still working in the arbor. I assumed there had been some disruption in the life of the nest, and suspected a possible source of trouble such as scavenger flies. Hornets are not always the best of housekeepers; remnants of food may accumulate in the bottom of the nest, with the flies then moving in to lay their eggs and rear a crop of maggots. There is also a parasitic wasp that may invade and destroy the hornet larvae.

Behavior of hornets and wasps is a mixture of the innate and the learned. Selection of the nest site, construction of the nest, and choice of prey vary little from generation to generation. Most insects never see their parents or their offspring. On the other hand, hornets learn the way to their nests, and remember the location of a caterpillar or other food they are unable to consume at one time.

This white-faced hornet is noted for its short temper. A friend was stung on the face by one of these insects and became quite ill, necessitating a hurried trip to the hospital. She had never known she was so allergic to the stings of hornets and their allies, wasps and bees.

Short-tailed Shrew

At one point in the boardwalk in Hatfield Swamp I found a short-tailed shrew that had apparently just been killed by a predator. At other times I have seen bodies of long-tailed shrews upon the walk, and have speculated that the creatures might have been dropped there by fox, mink, or hawk.

The shrew, smallest of North American mammals, is nauseous to most other animals, because it is provided with musk glands. Shrews are rarely eaten by beasts of prey, so the one in my path may have been left there by some mistaking predator.

The long-tailed shrew is of brownish color, but the short-tailed shrew, or *Blarina Brevicauda*, has much darker fur. It is so thick and velvety that some persons confuse the creature with a mole, despite its smaller size.

I tried to find the animal's eyes, but they were barely perceptible. They are believed to be of little use, except to distinguish light and dark. The shrew's sense of hearing and smell are highly developed, as is the sense of touch of its long whiskers.

Farther down the path I turned over a log and found one of the runways of the shrew, scarcely half an inch wide, and partly sunken in the mold and rotting vegetation. The runways lead to burrows, but themselves have little side chambers, filled with fine grasses for nests.

Cats in the Rocks

Manasquan Inlet is on the Jersey shore, lined with bulky chunks of traprock. It is a good place for horned grebes and red-throated loons, and, when dovekies are blown from the open sea, they are likely to be found at the inlet. One winter's day, when there I noticed at least six domestic cats running in and out of the great stones on the south side of the jetty. There were also plates of food that had apparently been left for the animals. I speculated that the cats were pets that had been abandoned by summer residents, and that some good Samaritan was helping them survive the winter.

Later I received a letter from the director of the New Jersey branch of the Humane Society of America saying my assumption was correct. "In this huge seashore area literally thousands of animals are left behind to fend for themselves when the summer residents go." She said that two kind women went to the rocks at the Inlet each night to place the food, and provided old blankets for beds. Another correspondent said that it is traditional for fishermen to share their catches with the cats. A local chapter of the Humane Society has established a shelter to help care for lost, strayed, and homeless small creatures in its area.

Eyes in the Dark

When we were driving home one night a deer walked across the road, and it seemed its eyes shone brilliant blue in the headlights. The scientists say, however, that animals' eyes do not actually shine in the dark, but that they merely reflect light shone into them. Their eyes do not have a light of their own; in complete darkness they do not shine.

Animals' eyes shine for somewhat the same reason that roadside reflectors do. Behind the retinas of creatures' eyes there is what amounts to a series of mirrors instead of a dark layer of pigment, as in the eyes of human beings.

The colors reflected from animals' eyes vary with the kind of beast. The greenish gleam of cats' eyes is familiar. Other animals show colors that range from silvery to blue-green, pale gold, reddish gold, brown, amber, and pink. Most resemble a reflection from a burnished metal surface. A study by the Smithsonian Institution said that the eyes of crocodiles and alligators gave the effect of "gazing into a brilliantly glowing pinkish opening in a dull-surfaced bed of coal." The study found no proof of the alleged shining of human eyes, although the most brilliant reflections were from the eyes of a kind of monkey, the lemur.

The reason that some animals' eyes gleam at night redder than others is said to depend upon the number and distribution of their blood vessels.

Red Bat

The red bat has been called the most beautiful of all American bats. It is reddish orange and its fur soft and fluffy. It is medium sized, 4 inches long with a wingspread of approximately a foot. I was surprised to see one of these creatures fly up from the path almost under my feet.

This bat has some of the characteristics of a bird. It does not seek shelter in gloomy caves and crevices, but hangs on trees and bushes in full light of the sun. Its tolerance of light enables it to start hunting insects earlier in the afternoon than other species in its range.

Red bats are known to migrate from the northern part of their range in September or October and return in May. One observer has recorded great flights of them down the Hudson Valley, lasting throughout the day. That they share the perils of migrating birds is indicated by observations on the New Jersey coast of individual bats coming in from the sea on September mornings, apparently exhausted from having strayed or being blown off their course.

Poisonous Snakes

Years ago I accompanied the Reptile Study Society of America on searches for rattlesnakes and copperheads in the rocky country around Hillburn, near Suffern, New York, which used to be called "Fifth Avenue of the Rattlers." Members of the society caught several of both species, and one of the favorite stunts was to hold the snake's fangs over the edge of a drinking glass whose top had been covered with gauze, and to see the brown venom trickle down the inside of the glass. This was a dangerous pastime, and one day a former head keeper of mammals and reptiles at the New York Zoological Garden in Bronx Park, New York City, was bitten by a rattler and died in spite of treatment at the hospital in nearby Suffern. In our state, rattlesnakes are found most frequently in the mountainous regions of the north and the Pine Barrens of the south. I have seen neither rattlesnake nor copperhead at Mt. Salem Farm. When during World War II I was stationed at Picatinny Arsenal, at the foot of Green Pond Mountain near Dover, both species were found in the hills which had long been protected from outsiders and had never been disturbed. The K-9 patrol dogs were bitten at times when they were patrolling with the guards at night. Nearby Pennsylvania still has snakes, and our North Hunterdon Rotary Club heard a snake hunter from Pennsylvania tell how he had killed 37 rattlers on one trip.

Our nearest encounter with a poisonous snake occurred one spring when a party of our friends was on a picnic to an area at Hibernia, which is near Picatinny. One of the girls was walking through a marshy area when she stepped over a log and onto a copperhead. The reptile bit her on the ankle, she screamed, and two of us rushed to her assistance. We helped her out of the marsh to the road, in order to prevent the poison circulating through her system more rapidly because of exercise, and when we reached the dirt road a physician, who happened to be in the party and who was the employer of the girl, gave her first aid: burning the end of his penknife to disinfect it, cutting light diagonals across the wound, and sucking out the poison. He also applied a tourniquet. Then two of us made a fireman's carry with our hands, and carried her up the hill to the car. We drove her to nearby Dover General Hospital, where she was injected with antivenin, and considered to be all right. However, for a month or more she suffered nervous reactions, and one day in scratching the wound dug out part of the snake's fang that was still imbedded there.

A curious part of the story was that when we returned to our host's home nearby, one of our party, who knew a local newspaper reporter, telephoned the account. This was early in the spring, probably the first snakebite story of the year, and the girl's employment was at a Park Avenue address in New York. The New York papers picked up the story, and it made an impression on the doctor's patients, who filled his secretary's office with sympathetic flowers. The doctor was mentioned in the story, and his friends in the profession began to twit him about being a snake doctor. But, as reputations are sometimes made, the word reached persons who did not understand the humor in it, and the doctor was asked to contribute a piece on the treatment of snakebite to a government publication and one day received a call from Chicago asking how to treat a particular case.

Suckers

A neighbor said the suckers in his pond were behaving in a curious way, so we went to look. The pond is fed by a brook which flows through a culvert. The suckers were gathered around the culvert, trying to ascend the water that was rushing from it.

Suckers spawn in the spring, leaving their habitat at the bottoms of shallow ponds and lakes to ascend the streams. There, on rocks or gravel shoals, each fish deposits some 50,000 eggs.

Suckers are strange fish. Those we saw were as much as 18 inches long, although they reach 30. This species was the white sucker, rather brownish white in color. The mouth is behind the point of the snout, and the lips are thick and suckerlike. The fish is a bottom feeder, consuming insects, mollusks, worms, and plant material.

This fish used to be a favorite of country boys, and I know some adults who relish a dish of suckers caught in early spring. My recollection is that the flesh tastes rather muddy and is filled with bones. Suckers may harbor internal parasites, so should be cooked thoroughly. The fish made their way up to our own brook, a quarter-mile away.

The white sucker is the variety most common from New England to the Columbia River. There are 75 species distributed among our lakes and streams; all are native to North America with the exception of 2 species found also in China. This strange distribution is explained by the hypothesis that the fish came north with the related carp from the tropical East, and crossed over to the continent by way of the Bering Sea when a land connection existed.

Dated Turtles

While cutting a nature trail along our brook we came upon two interesting crawling creatures, the box and the wood turtles.

The box turtle is our common species, and is probably the longest-lived of any form of American wildlife. It is approximately 6 inches long, the shell generally dark brown, decorated with numerous irregular yellow spots. The plastron is a uniform pale yellow. This lower shell is hinged near the middle, making two movable lobes that can be drawn up tightly against the upper shell. This provides a fortress that is probably impregnable to all of the enemies except man. However, it does not make the female impregnable to the male, for I have seen them copulating.

At home in open grasslands, pastures, and meadows, the box turtle feeds upon insects, grubs, worms, and fruit. At the peak of the wild strawberry season, which in our field is mid-June, it gets so fat that it cannot close its shells completely, so that when the forward shell is closed, the rear of the turtle is squeezed out at the back, and when that lobe is shut the creature's head and fore limbs are forced out.

Box turtles may live from thirty to sixty years, but there are reports of much greater longevity. Sometimes the evidence consists of dates and initials carved on the turtle's back, although this evidence may be of dubious validity.

A box turtle found in Hope Valley, Rhode Island, in 1953, bore the initials and dates EBK 1844 and GVB July 22, 1860. Searching in the area, Dr. James J. Oliver, then curator of reptiles at the Bronx Zoo, found in a cemetery the grave of Edward Barber Kenyon, with a headstone bearing the birth date of 1825. The deceased had lived half a mile from where the turtle was discovered. In 1947 the Willie Grout Post, Sons of Union Veterans of Worcester, Massachusetts, observed the death of Myrtle, a turtle that died in September that year in New Brunswick, New Jersey. The creature was believed to date back to the Civil War, because it had "Vicksburg, 1865" carved on its shell. (Vicksburg was invested in 1863.) In 1953 a man in North Scituate, Rhode Island, found a turtle in his garden with 1836 carved on its undershell.

The wood turtle is almost as terrestrial as the box turtle, although it is a good swimmer, and may be found in small brooks in the spring and fall. During the summer it prowls overland in woods and open grasslands, feeding upon tender vegetation and insects, earthworms and salamanders. In blueberry season its beak and forefeet may become heavily stained with the fruit.

At 8 inches, this is the largest of our turtles next to the snapping turtle, and in some localities its flesh is eaten. Its upper shell is dark brown, tinged with reddish. Each scale or shield is sculptured with many concentric ridges. The plastron is yellow with large patches of black. Head and limbs are dark brown above and brick-red beneath. The wood turtle is easily tamed, and learns to accept food from its owner's hand.

Fossil Remains

Occasionally an exciting discovery reminds us of our state's fascinating geologic history. One such discovery was in January 1962 when two teen-agers found mastodon teeth in an excavation near a gasoline station in Hackensack. Another, two years earlier, was when three Hudson County boys uncovered in Granton Quarry, West New York, the fossilized skeleton of a gliding reptile that may have been the first animal with a backbone ever to take to the air. The creature is believed to have traveled through trees like a flying squirrel some 175 million years ago.

New Jersey has been especially rich in remains of dinosaurs. In 1948 bones of a duck-billed dinosaur that roamed the coastal plains of the state some 60 million years ago were discovered near Sewell in Gloucester County. The beast was 30 feet long and resembled a giant lizard, walking on its hind legs and eating plants. At that time the coastal region of New Jersey was near the Delaware River, as much of the state was still covered with ocean. A century ago the first dinosaur skeleton to be found in the United States was dug up at Haddonfield, only a dozen miles from Sewell. In 1957 the thighbone of another duck-billed dinosaur was also unearthed in Gloucester County.

Remains of mastodons are also discovered with some frequency. In February 1954, for instance, a skeleton was found in the bottom of a pond in Vernon, Sussex County, when the pond was being enlarged. Six skeletons were found on a farm near Hackettstown many years ago.

New Jersey's geologic time chart goes back some three billion years to the pre-Cambrian era. Then there was much water and little land surface. The state did not really emerge from the sea until 300 million years ago in the Paleozoic era. One hundred million years or so later, lava flows created the Watchung Mountains and the Palisades, and dinosaurs were the dominant form of animal life. They roamed the earth for 140 million years. There were many kinds of these brutes, both plant eaters and flesh eaters, and some grew to be 80 feet long. The latest period has lasted 2 million years. In the Pleistocene epoch there were three great ice advances that covered New Jersey, depositing sands and gravels. Then there were in our area mammoths, mastodons, saber-toothed tigers, sloths, elks, and primitive horses. Man first appeared in the Pleistocene epoch.

When I was a boy in Rutherford I used to find many fossils in sand pits along the Passaic River. There was a certain rock with a hard exterior and soft interior that was rich in fossils and shells. There were impressions and remains of clams and scallops of several sizes, and once I found a fossil of what I believed was a trilobite, a strange creature that was the ancestor of all crustaceans.

Origin of Fishes

Once when I was walking in Hatfield Swamp I found a small pickerel in a puddle at least a half a mile from any water that normally would have supported pickerel. The incident puzzled me, but some light was thrown upon it by Robert Soldwedel in an article, "The Origin of Species," in an issue of *New Jersey*

Outdoors. He is with the Bureau of Fisheries Management in New Jersey.

Mr. Soldwedel mentions his bureau's experience with Spruce Run Reservoir, not far from my home in Pittstown. After it was drained, three species (rainbow trout, large-mouth bass, and alewife) were stocked. Today the reservoir's population consists of 23 species. Holmdel Park in Monmouth County and its drainage were reclaimed in October 1967 and subsequently stocked with trout. It was felt at the time that the reclamation had accounted for every fish. A population check the next summer turned up hundreds of sunfish, killifish, and goldfish, but no trout.

Mr. Soldwedel had several explanations as to how unwelcome fish get in. Most important is action of the public. Anglers discard unused bait fish into the pond. Youngsters release catfish and white perch in ponds that do not have these species. Flooding of adjacent waters may spread fish into a pond. Fish eggs may be carried on the feet of ducks or on the bottoms of boats and on fishermen's waders.

Chickaree

Possibly because of our pines, we see the red squirrel as well as the gray. Known also as the pine squirrel and the chickaree (because of its cry) it is only half the size of its gray relative. It, and its close relatives, can be found all over the United States and has a strong preference for coniferous woods.

It tries to climb our guarded bird feeders for sunflower seed, but has never succeeded, and it chews holes in the plastic containers we have in the garage for seeds. In the warm days of early spring we see it lying at full length along the tops of the branches of beeches along the brook, basking in the grateful warmth of the sun. Under one of the trees we came upon a great pile of pine cones, for since the creatures do not hibernate, they provide against the season of scarcity by accumulating these heaps of cones that sometimes contain 6 to 10 bushels. They are called middens. Each squirrel may live for years in or about a certain tree, and on the ground beneath may be found a large mound of discarded scales and centers of cones. Red squirrels are fond of edible mushrooms, and sometimes lay up a store among branches of trees or bushes to dry for winter use.

Although often described as vivacious and rollicking, the animal has one outstandingly bad characteristic. It eats eggs and young of small birds.

It is also said to be antagonistic to gray squirrels, although we notice infrequent encounters around our bird feeders. The great migrations of gray squirrels in 1933, 1935, 1937, and 1957 have been described by an authority writing in the official organ of the American Association for the Advancement of Science as the result of persecution by red squirrels. In those years the gray squirrels were seen to move from New England into New York State, swimming the Hudson River and crossing Bear Mountain Bridge. Hawks, owls, and foxes prey upon red squirrels, and this was said to have increased the population of grays to such an extent that the food supply became inadequate for both red and gray, so the more aggressive red squirrel drove out its relatives.

Star-nosed Mole

A neighbor telephoned that she had found a star-nosed mole near her pond, and I went down to see it. This is the only mole, indeed, the only mammal, with a star nose or a ring of 22 fleshy tentacles at the end of the nose which move as the animal searches for food. Our creature was about 4 inches long, its fur black, and its tail scaly with hairs thickest in the middle. It likes moist ground near water, makes mounds as much as a foot wide, and can swim and dive. Later, we found mounds of the mole on our lawn at Mt. Salem Farm, and later still one of the moles, dead.

Moles are sometimes killed on sight because they disfigure lawns and are believed to eat potatoes and other vegetables. However, there are few animals more valuable from the point of view of the agriculturist. They kill wireworms, cutworms, and other harmful insects, and do not eat vegetables. In France a fine is imposed upon anyone killing a mole.

Freshwater Sponges

I took a jar of water from our brook, including in it some dead leaves, and found freshwater sponges. It took a 450-power microscope to reveal the gemmules, minute dark balls of cells which are the only form in which most freshwater sponges live over the winter. The gemmules are stored with food yolk, and in the spring their cells multiply and form a sponge colony.

I found also the spicules, which are three-rayed needles of calcium carbonate that support the soft walls of the sponge. After mid-August the soft parts of the sponge colony disintegrate, leaving only the hard spicules and the gemmules attached to leaves or rocks.

8

PLANTS
AND PETALS

Wild Orchids

Of all the 53 species of wild orchids in New Jersey, the rarest is the small whorled pogonia, sometimes called the lesser five-leaved orchid (*Isotria medeoloides*). Some say it is the rarest in the East. Hence it was an exciting experience to find and photograph it one Memorial Day in a northern county. The good friends who discovered and told us of this plant swore us to secrecy, hence I cannot reveal (nor would I, anyway) the name of the place or the person. Orchids are so scarce in our state that to make their situations generally known would be to ensure their total disappearance. Orchid photographers constitute a kind of secret society.

The small whorled pogonia is a modest flower standing 6 to 8 inches high. Its stalk is gray-green and carries a circle of five light green leaves of the summit. The paired or solitary one-inch flowers are yellowish green, the lip bearing a broad crest and the sepals green. We found it in a dry oak woodland, in humus-rich soil.

A few miles away we were led by our guide to a rather substantial stand of the whorled pogonia, also called the five-leaved orchid (*Isotria verticillata*). This pogonia is also rare in the East, although not so unusual as its smaller relative. It stands 8 to 12 inches high. The stalk is purplish instead of green, and the sepals are 2 inches long, and madder-purple, the lip yellow, the petals greenish yellow.

In this general area were other interesting orchids; one was the showy. This is a delightful little orchid whose lavender and white flowers grow only 6 inches above the forest floor. Another was the familiar moccasin flower, and a third the related yellow lady's slipper. There were 140 of these blooms in one small area. We also came upon a small version of the yellow lady's slipper.

Another productive area for wild orchids is the Pine Barrens, which comprise some 2,000 square miles of land and pitch pine in the south-central part of the state. A good time to see them is early June. They like the acid bogs that are studded with white cedar and drained by small streams of tea-colored water. One day we found three, arethusa, grass pink, and rose pogonia.

Fairest of these is arethusa (*Arethusa bulbosa*), sometimes called Indian pink. It is named after Arethusa of Greek mythology, who was a nymph of the springs. This is a low plant, growing only 5 to 10 inches above the bog sand. The flowers are 1 to 2 inches long, magenta-crimson and with a delicate scent. Each bloom has a crest formed of three hairy ridges that are white or yellow, and has a lower lip spotted with magenta.

Another lovely orchid is the grass pink (*Calopogon pulchellus*). It grows almost twice as tall as arethusa, and carries three to nine magenta-pink flowers that are sweet scented. Each has a long spreading lip crested with yellow, orange, and magenta hairs. The third pink orchid and the most numerous was the rose pogonia (*Pogonia ophioglossoides*), also called gold-crest, snake-mouth, or beard flower. The last name is derived from the bearded lip of the species. The plant is from 8 to 13 inches tall, and the flower is pale crimson-pink. The sepals overhang a crested and fringed lip and are curved like the hollow of one's hand.

There were other fascinating and typical plants blooming in the Pine Barrens. One was turkey beard. It carries on the top of a stalk 2 to 3 feet high a dense cylinder of small white flowers. Another was the hoary pea. It grew in dense clumps, the flowers yellowish white marked with purple. While we were photographing the flowers, we were not oblivious to the prairie warblers that were singing on every side.

Orchids of the Pine Barrens are difficult to protect. There is actually nothing to prevent one from sending down a truck, digging them out to transport to a private bog. One such person in a nearby state did this, marking the plants for his truckers with green-tipped stakes. Conservationists counterattacked by roaming through the Barrens and pulling out all the green stakes they saw. Another hazard to the orchids is the sphagnum collector who digs it to sell commercially.

Needle Cast Fungus

One of the most attractive aspects of our farm has been its pines. We have approximately 12,000 evergreens, mostly Austrian pines and lesser numbers of white and Scotch pines and Norway spruces. Most of the Austrian pines are around 30 feet high, but some of the white pines reach 65 feet. The youngest pines are some eighteen years old and the oldest approximately thirty-three. From the beginning, however, the Austrian pines have suffered from being planted too closely together. They were planted this way so that in the thinning process some could be sold as Christmas trees. Now they do not get enough air and light.

Much to our distress we noticed four years ago that some of the Austrian pines seemed to be dying. Their needles were turning brown and dropping to the ground. This was in a cold, wet spring, the first of a succession, culminating in 1972 in a year with more rainfall than any other year on record in these parts. We asked Otto Kunkel, the area forester and an employee of the U.S. Department of Agriculture, to survey the situation. He did so, taking needles with him for study by his plant pathologist. The decision was that the disease afflicting the trees was "needle cast fungus," *Hypoderma lethale*, which is particularly bad in wet years. The remedy was that removal of diseased trees was the best control and that thinning and crop tree pruning to increase vigor was important. Not much is known about diseases of this tree in our area because there are very few Austrian pine plantations. Spraying is not recommended, because its effect is uncertain and its cost high.

At first the disease did not seem too rampant, but as the years went on and the cold, wet weather lingered, the situation began to appear desperate. In 1972 we began to fear we would lose the whole plantation of Austrian pines, although the other evergreens were not affected by the fungus. But how can you remove diseased trees when thousands of them appear to be affected?

We made a start, however. In New Jersey, and in other states, the U.S. Department of Agriculture maintained an Agricultural Stabilization and Conservation Service. In respect to our trees, this meant that the federal government agreed to pay us 80 percent of the cost of pruning and thinning the pines up to a certain limit, the pruning done in one year and the thinning the next. A man who often helps us with farm chores came over with his tractor and ropes, and I gave him our chain saw, and we went to work. (He did most of the work.) In the summer of 1972 we took down 125 trees, some of a diameter of 10 inches and more, dragged them down into our 5-acre field, cut off the branches and pulled the trunks to one side of the field.

We made six huge piles of branches, with the idea of burning them as soon as conditions seemed favorable. It was necessary to have a burning permit from the fire warden, a permit that lasted only three days, and we also asked the local fire department to come and stand by, in case the fire ran out of control. In such an exercise, you cannot pay the department for this service, but may contribute something to its general fund or supply a case of beer to the fire fighters. However, the weather was either so rainy or so windy throughout the rest of the year that we could never burn the brush, and on the first of the following January the state promulgated a regulation to the effect that no brush could be burned anywhere because of the adverse effect on air purity. Our friend Kunkel wrote that wood is a low-pollution fuel compared with oil, coal, and certain radioactive materials. It emits very little sulphur dioxide and no radioactive substances.

Another hazard to a pine plantation is weather, especially wind, ice, and snowstorms. We suffered a severe storm in March 1971 that damaged 63 of our trees, 46 Austrian pines, 12 white pines, 4 Scotch pines, and a tulip tree. The trees were damaged in various ways. Some were uprooted, others broken in half. Many were bent so severely that their tops almost touched the ground. These bent pines never straightened; it is best to cut them down. Most of them were a bit more than 21 feet tall. There is nothing that can be done with this wood. It would be possible to cut it into fireplace lengths and sell it from the end of our driveway, but this would be five times as costly as it would be worth. We burn some ourselves, but prefer hard wood.

This storm was so destructive because first there was a freezing rain, which coated the branches of the pines with ice an inch thick. On top of this came a heavy snow, and this was followed by winds of up to 50 miles an hour velocity. What tree could withstand such harassment?

We haven't quite given up on the burning of the dead trees, because they are diseased, and because the new state legislation allows burning as an exercise for a volunteer fire department. However, some of the pines, especially those along the county road where there is more air and light, seem to be reviving.

This is how the U.S. Department of Agriculture describes an

Austrian pine:

Pinus nigra. Medium-sized to large pyramidal cone-bearing evergreen tree with spreading branches and dense dark-green foliage. Bark dark gray, fissured into irregular, scaly plates. Needles two in cluster, 3½ to 6 inches long, dark green, stiff. Cones 2 to 3 inches long, yellow-brown, shiny, usually with short prickles. Several geographic and garden forms are distinguished. Native of central and southern Europe and Asia Minor and a valuable timber tree there. Across the United States one of the commoner foreign ornamental trees. Used also in shelterbelts. Hardy in East, extending north to southern New England and in West except coldest, hottest, and driest regions. Grows in sandy loam and dry soils. Tolerant of city dust and smoke.

Walnuts

I have just finished cracking some black walnuts that we gathered from trees on our property, and it was high time I did, because the tasty meats were getting a bit dry and lacked the juiciness they possessed earlier.

To open the nuts easily, first spread them in the warm sun until the husks are soft, even slightly rotten, and can be removed easily. Let the nuts dry. Then place in a moderate oven, about 350 degrees, for about fifteen minutes, or until the shells open a crack. Using a hard surface, such as a flat stone, lay the nuts with one seam down and tap the upper seam on the edge with a hammer. Be careful to pick the nutmeats carefully, as it is easy to overlook a small bit of shell.

Priscilla uses the meats with caramelized sugar and grated orange rinds for an excellent candy. Our neighbor, Laura Riley, brought us some quince conserve the other day. She had added walnut meats to it for a surprising and desirable ingredient.

It was timely, therefore, to receive from Mrs. Charles Reed of Piscataway a document which substantiates her own observations of a certain antagonism between the many black walnuts that grow on her own land and other trees and shrubs. The document comes from the Agricultural Experiment Station of West Virginia University. It reports field studies of 300 black walnut trees in Vest Virginia, Maryland, Ohio, and Michigan. Data are given for the frequency of occurrence, both within and beyond the root spread of walnut trees, of 63 tree species, 35 shrubs and vines, and 123 herbaceous plants. Observations are also given on apparent antagonisms between black walnut trees and apple, potato, tomato, alfalfa, blackberry, heaths, and other plants.

Evidence concludes that black walnut trees exert a detrimental effect upon certain other plants, as red pines and rhododendron, that grow within the walnut's root spread. This spread is a 60-foot radius, approximately a quarter acre, surrounding each tree. Black walnuts produce a substance that is often toxic to other plants. It is possible that this is juglone, a naphtha-quinone. However, evidence also indicated that actual contact with walnut roots is necessary before associated plants are harmed.

Big Trees

An engaging business is to keep track of the biggest trees. One day, for instance, I received the "List of New Jersey's Biggest Trees" from Rutgers University and a few days later the "Social Register of Big Trees," compiled by the American Forestry Association and appearing in an issue of *American Forests.*

The first was a list of all big trees in our state, but the AFA's list was just the 117 that had been added that year to an earlier comprehensive list of all the biggest trees in the country. Constant changes must be made as some of the old champions succumb to the forces of nature or to residential and commercial developments, or as new bigger trees are discovered.

The New Jersey bulletin says the state's biggest tree is a white oak, 21½ feet in circumference, growing near Cream Ridge in Monmouth County. In respect to possession of the biggest trees, Mercer County leads with 17; Burlington is second with 14.

My own county, Hunterdon, can boast of only two champions, a black birch and white walnut. Most of the Mercer County trees are in Princeton, and I surmise they have survived because that community has always been careful to protect its environment.

The list of New Jersey's biggest trees includes 78. I was especially interested in a cucumber tree, a kind of magnolia, that is 14 feet in circumference and grows in a yard at 652 Bloomfield Avenue in Caldwell and was nominated by the Friendly Ice Cream Company. When we lived in that community we admired and photographed it. Incidentally, all circumference measurements are made at a point 4½ feet above ground.

It was impossible to compare the two lists, but I noted that the new national cucumber tree (*Magnolia acuminata*) in Longwood Gardens, Pennsylvania, has a circumference of only 10 feet 11 inches, whereas our cucumber tree in Caldwell has a girth more than 3 feet greater.

One of my readers, noting that our county boasted the largest white walnut in the state, asked to know more about this tree. The specimen was said to be 5 feet 2 inches in circumference, and situated in the front yard of the Henry Zebuhr farm in Lebanon Township. It is noted in both the "List of New Jersey's Biggest Trees" and in the "Social Register of Big Trees."

The white walnut (*Juglans cinerea*) is also called the butternut tree. It is close kin to the black walnut. The bark is ashy gray and separates into wide flat ridges. Leaves are alternate, compound, with 13 to 23 leaflets. Fruit is an elongated nut with a hairy, sticky, nonsplitting husk. It is pointed at one end and has four ribs. Inside is a sweet, oily, edible meat. The white walnut or butternut is common locally in northern New Jersey, extending southward to Burlington, Mercer, and Middlesex counties.

Later I received a letter from Mrs. Dorothy Zebuhr saying that her champion butternut or white walnut tree I had mentioned was (in 1971) 6 feet 6 inches in circumference, and that the measurement of 5 feet 2 inches given in the "List of New Jersey's Biggest Trees" was taken several years before. The tree is in good health, she said, and the only aid she gives is to let the hose trickle on its roots in dry weather.

However, competition appeared almost immediately. Mrs. John Van Saun of Midland Park wrote that she had a butternut in her yard that had a circumference of 6 feet 8 inches.

Osage Orange

Under the bright yellow leaves of the Osage oranges that grow as a hedge around part of our field, we find early in November the lime-yellow fruit in profusion on the ground. These oranges, or apples as they are sometimes called, are 3 to 5 inches in diameter, with a pebbly surface. When you cut into them you find a mass of seeds, and your knife is covered with a white, sticky juice that comes off the blade only when rubbed with steel wool. They are not edible, although cattle may chew them in drought years. They cannot chew the oranges thoroughly because cows have small teeth. When swallowed partially whole, the oranges stick in the throats of the beasts and may prove fatal if not detected in time. We have noted that deer also chew them.

The Osage orange flourishes in Kansas and Oklahoma. These tough, thorny trees were popular as hedges and their use for this purpose spread over much of the United States. In Kansas a bill was passed in 1867 which provided a bounty of two dollars for each four rods of fence that would resist stock, as fencing material was a problem for settlers. This promoted the popularity of the tough Osage orange. The Osage Indians made bows from the wood, as it is tough and pliable.

Mulberry Tree

A center of attraction for birds at Mt. Salem Farm is a red mulberry tree not far from my study. It is a small specimen, some 20 feet high, although occasionally the trees reach 60 feet or more. The dark purple blackberrylike fruit is less than an inch long, juicy and cloyingly sweet. This tree is widely cultivated in the Southern states, as its fruit is an esteemed food for pigs and poultry. When I was a boy in Alabama we had a huge red mulberry in our yard; it blanketed the ground with its fruit.

Most birds eat mulberries, and 48 species have been known to feed on the red. We have seen robin, kingbird, Baltimore oriole, grackle, and goldfinch eating the fruit. Woodpeckers also like mulberries.

When we lived in Caldwell we had a white mulberry tree in our yard, and it also attracted birds. A friend in New Vernon said that at the moment of her writing a white mulberry in her yard was being visited by five goldfinches, two Baltimore orioles, three catbirds, a brown thrasher, and two robins. The white mulberry is smaller than the red and is an imported species, brought from China to provide food for silkworms. It is now more or less naturalized. In my opinion, the fruit is inferior in taste to that of the red mulberry.

Bowman's Hill

If you want an exciting time with wildflowers, visit Bowman's Hill Wildflower Preserve at Washington Crossing State Park in Pennsylvania. We spent some time there one day in May, but realized we should have devoted the whole day. The preserve is 2¹/₂ miles west of New Hope on Route 32. Its hundred acres were set aside by the park commission in 1934 to be developed as a sanctuary for flowers, trees, shrubs, and ferns native to Pennsylvania.

Success of this development is seen in the species of plants now in the preserve. They include flowering plants, more than 600; trees, 85; shrubs, 84; vines, 30; grasses, 21; ferns and club mosses, 70. The plants are found along 22 trails that range in length from 150 to 1,250 feet and are given descriptive names, such as azalea, bluebell, fern, marsh marigold, gentian. Labels with botanical and common names are on plantings along the trails.

This is a splendid way to become acquainted with plants that are around one's own home and which may be hard to identify. For instance, we are confused by violets because we have never studied them sufficiently. Of the approximately 100 species of violets native to the United States, around 30 have been determined as native to Pennsylvania, and all but one of these are either present naturally in the preserve or have been established there. On Marshmarigold Trail, for instance, we found in bloom the downy yellow, halberd-leaved yellow, smooth yellow, American dog, cream, stone, and common violets. As violets may vary widely in habitat requirements, they cannot all be grown along one trail, but are planted according to their needs. This year the best time to see violets was between April 28 and May 4.

If you go to Bowman's Hill on a Sunday, allow plenty of time to get home. Routes 32 and 202 converge at the narrow bridge over the Delaware River between New Hope and Lambertville, and weekends see massive traffic jams. It took us an hour and twenty minutes to cover the 2¹/₂ miles from the preserve to the bridge.

Pine Barrens Gentian

A steadfast effort to save the Pine Barrens gentian from destruction has been conducted for the last few years by Mrs. Neil Knorr of New Shrewsbury.

Her interest began when she joined a field trip to the Pine

Barrens and found none of the gentians at Atsion, where they have always grown. A few weeks later she and Mr. Knorr returned and were horrified to find that a highway mowing machine had just preceded them and mangled three of the rare plants. She took them home, nurtured them carefully, and next year they bore 13 flowers that set seed.

Mrs. Knorr planted the seed in 25 containers, encouraged their growth with artificial lights, and protected them from fungus, nematodes, and toxic soil poisoning. When the tiny gentians were put in her nursery, she guarded them from squirrels, cottontails, slugs, aphids, beetles, and other pests. Grackles and starlings nevertheless uprooted many seedlings. That fall she offered many of her hundreds of surviving gentians to public arboretums, sanctuaries, and wildflower preserves.

The Pine Barrens gentian (*Gentiana autumnalis*) lives in the damp sand in the Barrens and in the southern part of Cape May peninsula. Its flaring mouth, delicate markings within, and the intensity of its blue make it one of the choicest blooms of the region. It was first discovered by William Bartram (1739–1823), famed ornithologist and botanist. It grows from the Pine Barrens to Virginia and the southeast.

Diatoms

Underlying shallow deposits of peat in a number of swamps and meadows in northern New Jersey is what is called diatomaceous earth. This is soft, chalky, light material that is found in some degree all around the world, and in our country chiefly in Oregon, Washington, Nevada, Florida, and New York, as well as in New Jersey. Some of this earth has been dug for use in the manufacture of polishing powders, concrete, dynamite, and filters for cane sugar, fruit juices, and other beverages.

Deposits of diatomaceous material were formed under water in past geologic times and are now found where the seas have receded. They are composed of the skeletons of innumerable minute algae called diatoms. More than 16,000 species are known, and these are found in fresh and salt water and in moist soil. These plants have cell walls that are composed largely of silica, a hard, flinty substance that is a constituent of sand. When the aquatic forms die they drop to the bottom, and the shells, not being subject to decay, collect in the ooze and form diatomaceous earth.

Diatoms are equisitely beautiful under the microscope. They resemble minute glass boxes in innumerable shapes and designs. I saw several forms, one that was shaped like a canoe, one like a grain of corn, a third like a dime with an interior design, and still another like a small rectangle, the rectangles occurring sometimes in strings.

Wild Strawberries

A pleasant time of the year arrives when wild strawberries ripen, and they were perfect in our field at the end of the first week in June. Fortunately, this was also a day when four of our grandchildren were here, in ages from two to seven, and they had great fun gathering the fruit, competing to see who could find the most. Three of them dropped their strawberries into paper cups and added ice and sugar to make what they called soda, but two-year-old Lisa would have none of this, insisting upon eating her fruit plain, so finally her face and even her forehead were stained pink. You see such a stain sometimes on the faces and feet of wood turtles that also relish wild strawberries.

Picking wild strawberries is best as a family pastime, and my brother and his wife from Kansas and Priscilla and I gathered a generous quantity next day, using sticks to part the other plants in our field and to avoid poison ivy. We brought home our harvest, added an equal part of sugar and allowed the fruit to cook in the sun and make the most delectable of all strawberry jams.

Thinking about wild strawberries, I wondered what others had written. I scanned several of the relaxed, journal-type of books, such as William Beebe's *The Log of the Sun,* Ernest Ingersoll's *Nature's Calandar,* Hal Borland's *Sundial,* Leonard Hall's *Country Year,* Eva Rodimer's *The Year Outdoors,* and even George H. Ellwanger's *Idyllists of the Countryside.* I found nothing in these books about wild strawberries. None has an index, so perhaps I did not look carefully enough.

Butterfly Weed

What good is it if you have butterfly weed but no butterflies? Three years ago we dug two spindly plants from our field, barely a foot high, and planted them near my study. Now we have a stand that is 6 feet long, a yard high, and displays some 500 clusters of orange-yellow blossoms.

This species of milkweed is not so milky as that of other varieties, but the blossoms are proverbially attractive to butterflies. One writer lists a dozen species hovering over the plant. However, I do not see many butterflies of any species on our flowers.

I suspect this is not because the flowers lack beauty, but because the population of butterflies has been cut down so radically by the use of pesticides and the destruction of their habitats. While I was counting the blossoms and lamenting the lack of winged insects, a male ruby-throated hummingbird hovered within an arm's length, so all was not lost.

Poor Acorn Crops

Why so few acorns and jays? I had noticed the small number of jays the past winter and attributed it to a poor acorn crop. Otto Kunkel, our district forester, stopped by the other day to look at our plantation and I mentioned acorns. Mr. Kunkel has also noticed their scarcity, and it worries him.

He says that in north and central New Jersey especially, oak trees are not reproducing themselves so well as in the past, and he believes this is because of poor seed reproduction. He has tried to collect acorns many times without success. For seed collecting he must go to parks, lightly wooded pastures, or woodlots that were formerly grazed and where he finds widely spaced dominant oaks with large crowns.

Mr. Kunkel believes that the answer to the problem is that woodlands are too crowded. He has explored the matter with others, among them Silas Little, principal silviculturist of the Forest Service's experimental station in Upper Darby, Pennsylvania. The latter believes that the oaks have suffered from competition and increased shade from other hardwood trees, especially sugar maples in recent years, resulting in denser understories and overstories in the woodlands. He adds that the situation has been aggravated by fewer forest fires, longer lives for the trees because fuelwood is no longer a major product, and recovery of density because of the disappearance of chestnuts.

Mr. Kunkel believes that a program of thinning trees is desirable, as it will produce healthy and vigorous remaining trees that are more resistant to drought, disease, and insects.

Christmas Trees

The pleasure of living in the country is heightened by Yuletide. One of our rites is to invite our family and a few old friends to visit us and cut their own Christmas trees.

One Sunday in the midst of a snowstorm, two couples and their children arrived, bringing with them Italian bread, cheese, and red Bordeaux wine. They also brought a pot of Chinese soup that one had made from ingredients procured from a shop in New York's Chinatown. It was very agreeable to taste all this before the fireplace while outside the pines were being heavily laden with snow and the birds fed actively on sunflower seeds and suet.

Vermont officials are armed with a new state law that makes it illegal to go out in the woods and chop down a Christmas tree wherever it may be found. The law requires that anyone transporting a tree or evergreens must have with him a bill of sale. The law considers the tree stolen unless a person can prove he bought it or cut it with the consent of the property owner. Maximum penalty is six months in jail and a three-hundred-dollar fine.

9

BECOMING A BIRDER PAINLESSLY

The easiest way to become a bird watcher is to place feeders on windowsills or in places in your yard where they can be seen from windows. Our house is new and has no windowsills, although we found a type of simple tray feeder very desirable when we lived in our previous old house. It was easy to replenish and afforded intimate views of visiting birds.

The classic story of bird watching from a window is Ada Clapham Govan's *Wings at My Window,* published in 1940 and in its fifteenth printing by 1947 when I bought it. Assailed by personal misfortunes and finally by an injury which resulted in arthritis in hip and spine, she faced the life of a housebound invalid. One day a chickadee appeared at her window, and this started an interest in birds that revived her spirits and even cured her arthritis. At the end she had saved the nearby woodlands

from destruction and had established a sanctuary. It is a senti-
mental story, but many thousands loved it.

I know what window feeders mean to women because my
column on outdoors in the *Newark Sunday News* was read by
many housewives, and often their only contact with nature was to
see it through window glass. Generally these were kitchen
windows. One of our lovely neighbors near our old house had six
children, and it seemed to me that she was always in the kitchen. I
received innumerable letters from these readers, telling of creatures that appeared in their yards and at their feeders, as pine
siskins one year, or an occasional bird that was partly albinistic,
or early- or late-feeding cardinals, or the scarcity of jays or
juncos in a particular year. Certainly the experience added a
valuable dimension to their lives, and my wife and I enjoyed
reading their letters at day's end.

Through Glass Doors

Old houses never seem to look outward. Our previous home
was built in 1890, and was not open and airy. When we envisaged
our house at Mt. Salem Farm in 1964 we asked an old acquaintance and exceptionally gifted architect to plan it. He lived
in North Caldwell, but had designed many houses for places on
Cape Cod. We took him to our house and to three prospective
sites for a new home, and by that time he understood our way of
life and our interest in the outdoors. His plans were ideal for our
needs: exposure to the south and west; large doors of plain glass
(thermopane) in study and kitchen, both on the southwest, and
doors even in our bedroom looking down a fire lane to the south.
Our site was in a dense evergreen plantation, but next to the
county road. We had to cut out 70 pines to make a space for the
house. I worry whether the pines are too near the house in case
the whole plantation catches fire, but the insurance company says
that a distance of 50 feet is sufficient protection, in spite of the

fact that there are some 12,000 pines in the plantation. I still worry.

Since the house is a modified Cape Cod colonial, it is built close to the ground, so we need only to slide the glass doors in the study, for instance, and we are outside. The chief advantage is that the outdoors is never closed to us. In the kitchen, where we take our breakfast and luncheon, we sit at a large circular pine table next to six-by-six feet of glass. It is a constant pleasure to look out on the birds feeding.

Types of Feeders

In order to have the best views we had to put up feeders. The simplest is a half-cocoanut. I cut three in half with a metal saw, scraped out the meat, and bored three holes around each cut rim. I inserted thin wire through the holes and hung the feeders from both the wooden top of the patio that runs from our kitchen to garage, and the branches of nearby trees. We put sunflower seeds in the nuts, and this winter these feeders have been visited by at least 20 purple finches and a smaller number of evening gros-beaks. American goldfinches, chickadees, both species of nut-hatches, and titmice are also frequent visitors.

Our principal feeders visible from the house are two that I constructed of redwood, and although I was hesitant about using this precious wood, I found it available at the lumberyard and knew it would be easy to work and would resist the weather. Each of these feeders is 2 feet wide and 10 inches deep, with a roof. I fastened each box to an iron pole approximately $7^{1}/_{2}$ feet long with a metal flange. On the poles I affixed, approximately a half foot under each box, a conical baffle that I had made at a local metalworking shop. It has a diameter of a foot and a half.

These feeders are absolutely squirrelproof. But what of their movability? One is fastened to a sturdy base of heavy boards that I can move from place to place. The other sits in a cement base, but can be pulled out for cleaning or repair. I dug a square hole some two feet deep, made a wooden form to fit it, and while Priscilla held the pole in place I poured in the cement. I allowed the cement to set a little and then pulled out the pole. The result is a receptacle in which I can leave the pole and feeder or take it out as becomes necessary.

Suet Feeder

We have had a bit of trouble with suet feeders because of the raccoons. If the containers are made of wire (we call it "hardware cloth"), the creatures demolish them or even take them away. What we did finally was to affix to the top of one of our iron poles a discarded metal milk-bottle carrier. These are $1^1/_2$ feet long by 10 inches deep and 10 inches high. The metal is very strong, and no raccoon could tear it apart. I place a board and a stone on the open top and cover the pole itself with heavy motor grease. We have relatively little problem at our suet station now.

We put sunflower seeds in the feeders I have mentioned, but it is also desirable to scatter feed on the ground. Juncos and sparrows are ground feeders. One of our stations is a large slab of stone, such as is used for walks. We also spread seed in our driveway, which is covered with crushed stone and which may supply grit also for our guests. We throw mixed birdseed and cracked corn for the ground-feeding birds. A neighbor who manages a pony farm sometimes gives us buckets of corn on the cob that is somewhat moldy. This corn is used for pony food, but when it gets a bit mildewed it is no longer suitable. There are plenty of good kernels for the birds, however; we throw out the whole cobs and soon they are picked clean. Pheasants and mourning doves are especially fond of this fare. In the winter we have an electric immersible heater to keep the water in the bird baths open.

Plantings That Attract Birds

I believe we find as much pleasure in the birds that feed on our Washington thorn tree or in our red mulberry as sometimes we derive from the feeders. The Washington thorn is a constant joy. We planted it six years ago when it was barely 3 feet high, and now it is 15 feet. It has long thorns, and is covered heavily in the fall with red, succulent berries. These berries persist as long as the birds will allow, because the creatures consume them greedily. We have counted evening grosbeaks, purple finches, catbirds, cedar waxwings, robins, mockingbirds, and numerous other species in the tree. Most of the berries are gone by early March. Fortunately the tree is only a dozen feet from my study windows. The Washington thorn is so-called because it was believed that the nation's capital was the normal northern limit of its range. However, it does well in New Jersey. Occasionally we visit friends in Washington who live near Rock Creek Park, and we see the streets lined with the trees, where it is a favorite ornamental species. Our friends say that in the fall cedar waxwings work up and down the streets, feeding on the berries.

Our red mulberry attracts as many species, including the catbird, robin, mockingbird, Baltimore oriole, cardinal, and purple finch. This tree is only a few feet behind the Washington thorn and was here when we arrived, although it has prospered since we have cleared around it. I don't know of any data on the subject, but I suspect that the white mulberry that was in our yard in Caldwell lures more birds. This species was introduced into this country from China to serve as a host plant to silkworm moths.

There are many other kinds of plants on our farm that were here when we came and which attract birds. The Fish and Wildlife Service has listed species most useful to birds, and anyone wishing to make plantings should get the government bulletins. At Mt. Salem Farm we were fortunate to find when we bought the land that it was rich in dogwood trees, as they make it very pleasant in the spring with their white petals and equally beautiful in the fall with their bronze-red foliage. Some 98 species of birds are said to like the red fruit. However, there were many other plants here, also beloved of birds, like sassafras trees, where the kingbirds feed on berries in the fall, and spicebush, greenbrier, Virginia creeper, and numerous others. We introduced plants that also provide food for birds, such as various kinds of yew, ilex, and viburnum.

Membership in Bird Clubs

Once a person has developed a slight interest in birds by feeding or planting shrubs or trees that they like, he can join a bird club to help him make a more active approach. The easiest is to join a local bird club, such as the Hunterdon County Bird Club or the Morris Nature Club, where the meetings are monthly and the dues three dollars a year. There are few demands upon the members of these clubs. They arrive from short distances each month to hear and see color slide presentations about birds and flowers of their area, or the region, presented by members of the club or by others who live nearby. Sometimes these are excellent, but the fee paid to the guest speaker is little or none. The members have no real obligation to help; they may be asked in the course of the meeting to contribute observations of what they have seen during the past month, and sometimes these notes produce unusual sightings.

In these smaller clubs there are often persons to take an active participation in Christmas bird counts and various field trips, but, unless the average age is kept down, there is a tendency for the older members to slough off an active participation and attend the meetings merely to be entertained. I know of one rather venerable club that reached this stage, and cancelled its Christmas count one year because nobody had the energy to go out in the cold weather.

Probably the major demand upon members of these clubs is to participate in the Christmas bird count; sometimes they go afield, and in other cases report what they have seen at their feeders. The success of the programs depends upon a dedicated person who will arrange a schedule of speakers, and upon another who will organize, lead, and compile the annual Christmas bird count, without which nothing! I do not believe, however, that the average bird-club member is more lethargic than the average garden-club member. Names of local bird clubs can be obtained from the National Audubon Society, 1130 Fifth Avenue, New York, New York, 10028.

Between the local bird club and the august American Ornithologists' Union, there are associations of bird watchers in many degrees of activity, dedication, and contribution. The Urner Ornithological Club of Newark was once a fire-eating association (no women as members) that made many contributions of species and numbers seen here and there. Even this organization tends to have a higher age level, and the leaders of yore are either gone or no longer eager for heroic Big Days in May. The Delaware Valley Ornithological Club, based in Philadelphia, has been able to maintain its vigor, and the Linnaean Society of New York may not have changed much. It is an organization composed of staff members of the American Museum of Natural History, where its meetings are held, and of accomplished mature birders from the New York area, and beginners. Many of the best birders in the New York area have begun with the Linnaean. It has biweekly meetings, field trips, and an annual meeting.

State Organizations

The state birding organizations are very helpful. Largest of these is Massachusetts Audubon Society, but I am more familiar with the New Jersey organization. It has some 3,600 members, and conducts trips periodically to such fine New Jersey areas as

Cape May, Brigantine National Wildlife Refuge, and the Pine Barrens. I have seen a thousand persons at the Society's annual meeting in Cape May. The Society publishes a quarterly magazine, *New Jersey Nature News,* and in a recent issue Maurice Chaillet, the president, wrote of the relationship between bird watching and conservation:

> Our constitution immediately places conservation with the prime objectives and aims of our Society. In the beginning, 62 years ago, this meant the saving from extinction of a few species as egrets and herons. Quickly it was evident that to save them we must provide space with sanctuary from the pressures of man.
>
> The conservationist, faced with the extinction of increasing numbers of plants and animals, was for a long time alone; his was an often unrewarded effort to preserve the threatened and provide a living space for them. He sensed the effects of deteriorating environment upon the life within its boundaries, but there was little positive reaction to the mounting evidence.
>
> Gradually, garden clubs, nature clubs, and bird clubs formed. They found their ultimate aims often overlapped, and conservation with its many facets emerged as their unifying theme. Our Society now has many affiliated clubs. This has been a happy union which has created a center where the local clubs may find assistance with their projects and the benefit of our Society's experience. Conversely, the union of these clubs under the Society's leadership has formed a consolidated front in the many causes of conservation. We look to this continued communication as an implement to conserve and maintain a healthy, enjoyable, and safe environment for our survival and the mutual benefit of all.

National Groups

Next you come to the great national organizations, such as the National Audubon Society, the American Ornithologists' Union, and the Wilson Ornithological Club. The individual member receives the society's publications and may attend its annual meetings. They are strong forces for conservation, especially the National Audubon Society. This society publishes *Audubon Magazine,* now devoted largely to conservation, and *American Birds,* which is concerned mainly with birds and climaxes its efforts each year with an issue which contains complete reports on the annual Christmas counts, an issue which in 1972 contained 550 pages.

The American Ornithologists' Union publishes *The Auk,* a magazine concerned chiefly with current research in ornithology and a bit too technical for the average birder. It also publishes at long intervals "The A.O.U. Check-List of North American Birds." The fifth edition came out in 1957. The checklist is the authority on nomenclature, spelling, type localities, range of birds, casual and accidental occurrences. The 1957 edition covered 1,684 species and subspecies, and its scope was North America north of Mexico, with inclusion of Greenland, Bermuda, and Baja California. The AOU holds an annual meeting in a good birding area; the 1968 session was at Fairbanks, Alaska.

In 1973 the AOU checklist committee issued a supplement to the 1957 checklist, listing some of the changes that will be required in the next edition of the AOU checklist. One of the changes is to extend the coverage of the next checklist to all of geographic North America, including Middle America and the West Indies. Another is to lump together what have been separate species, as to eliminate the names myrtle warbler and Audubon's warbler in favor of just the one, yellow-rumped warbler.

In addition to the general types of bird organization, there are specialized kinds, like the bird-banding associations.

It is obvious that the person interested in birds receives different kinds of help from different organizations. Probably the most rewarding is the local bird club, because not only does he become acquainted with others in his community who are birders, but he also grows familiar with the places to find birds and learns something more about the creatures' habits and occurrence.

Books about Birds

The beginner is lost without field guides. These are either general, in that they describe all birds in the United States, or specific, as relating to the birds of Texas, for instance. Everyone requires a general guide, but there is not so much reason to own a guide to the birds of Texas unless one lives there or expects to go there. Instead of listing miscellaneous bird books, I shall put down here only some in my library that have proved useful and, in fact, indispensable, because the relevance of the reference work to my needs must be apparent by now.

Field Guides

A Field Guide to the Birds, by Roger Tory Peterson, Houghton Mifflin Company, Boston, 1947. Second revised and enlarged edition, 290 pp., plus 36 color plates, 22 plates in black and white. A popular guide to birds found east of the Rockies, with each species identified with text that describes field marks, voice, and range. In both text and pictures the distinctive field marks are emphasized. End papers show silhouettes of birds.

A Field Guide to Western Birds, by Roger Tory Peterson, Houghton Mifflin Company, Boston, 1961. Second revised and enlarged edition, 366 pp., plus 28 line sketches and 60 plates. This book gives field marks of all species found in North America west of the one-hundredth meridian, with a section on the birds of the Hawaiian Islands.

Audubon Bird Guide, by Richard H. Pough, Doubleday & Company, Inc., Garden City, New York, 1949, 312 pp., 48 color plates. There is little to choose between this and Peterson's guide; both have sold hundreds of thousands of copies.

Audubon Western Bird Guide, by Richard H. Pough, Doubleday & Company, Inc., Garden City, New York, 1957. Concerns the land, water, and game birds of western North America, including Alaska, from Mexico to the Bering Strait and the Arctic Ocean. Thirty-two pages of color illustrations by Don Eckelberry and line drawings by Terry M. Shortt.

Birds of North America, by Chandler S. Robbins, Bertel Bruun, and Herbert S. Zim, illustrated by Arthur Singer, Golden Press, New York, 1966. Many birders prefer this book to the Peterson and Pough guides because it includes in one volume, instead of two or three, all the species on the continent of North America, or some 645 breeding species. Maps accompany the description of each species, showing the winter range, the summer or breeding range, and areas where the bird occurs all year. The book includes song diagrams which enable the user of the book to visualize the approximate pitch of a song, the quality, the phrasing, the tempo, the length of individual notes, and the entire song.

A Field Guide to the Birds of Texas, text and illustrations by Roger Tory Peterson, Houghton Mifflin Company, 1960, 304 pp., 20 line illustrations, 60 plates. Texas has more species of birds than any other state, 540, or nearly as many as have been listed in all Europe west of the Iron Curtain. The Pecos River is the dividing line between species that are typically those of the East and those of the West. The state is so big that it deserves a field book of its own.

A Field Guide to the Birds of Britain and Europe, by Roger Tory Peterson, Guy Mountfort, and P. A. D. Hollom, Houghton Mifflin Company, Boston, 1954, 318 pp., 16 line illustrations, 64 plates. The book covers all the birds of Britain and all those found this side of Russia. There are maps showing the breeding and winter ranges of the species.

Birds of Europe, by Bertel Bruun and Arthur Singer, McGraw-Hill Book Company, New York, 1970, 319 pp., with 2,000 full-color illustrations of 516 species by Arthur Singer. Every known species, including the birds of European Russia, is pictured and described. Distributional maps show the breeding and wintering ranges.

Where to Find Birds

In addition to guides that help in identification of birds, the beginner needs books that tell him where to go. Two books supply this need, but they are rather dated now, and the description of what routes to take and so on may be superseded. However, the area usually does remain, and if the birder cannot get there one way he can try another and perhaps better route.

A Guide to Bird Finding East of the Mississippi, by Olin Sewall Pettingill, Jr., Oxford University Press, New York, 1951, 659 pp. This book, which contains numerous line sketches of birds by George Miksch Sutton, is divided into chapters according to states. Each state's best birding areas are listed alphabetically, and specific instructions are given on how to get to each place and the birds that will be found there. This volume covers the 26 states lying entirely east of the Mississippi River.

A Guide to Bird Finding West of the Mississippi, by Olin Sewall Pettingill, Jr., Oxford University Press, New York, 1953, 709 pp. Sutton also does the incidental line drawings of birds for this volume. The book is identical in its organization and style with the volume on bird finding in the East. Twenty-two western states are covered.

The Bird Watcher's America, edited by Olin Sewall Pettingill, Jr., McGraw-Hill Book Company, New York, 1965, 441 pp., with incidental illustrations by John Henry Dick. This is a kind of sequel to the guides to bird finding, but is composed of pieces of notable environments written by 46 contributors. Howard L. Cogswell writes about the California chaparral country, for instance, and George Miksch Sutton describes the Black Mesa Country of Oklahoma. The book cuts the country into regions, with essays of 2,500 words on each.

Life Histories

The comprehensive work on detailed life histories of birds is *Life Histories of North American Birds* by Arthur Cleveland

Bent, United States National Museum, Washington, D.C. Mr. Bent's great cooperative enterprise began in 1919, and by 1953 he had completed 19 volumes. These volumes could be procured, when published, from the United States Government Printing Office for prices ranging from 50 cents to $4.50. However, the supply of each was soon exhausted, so that they could be obtained only in secondhand bookstores. Dover Publications, New York, has reprints at a cost of from $2.50 to $5.00, depending upon the size of the volume. Text is practically as in the original, but there are fewer illustrations. Mr. Bent died in 1954, when he had published 19 volumes and had finished the accounts of the icterids (blackbirds, orioles, tanagers) for volume 20, which was seen through the press in 1958 by Mr. Bent's literary successor, Wendell Taber, of the Nuttall Ornithological Club of Cambridge. Taber died in 1960, but shortly before his death asked Oliver L. Austin, Jr., of the Florida State Museum in Gainesville, Florida, to assume his life-history responsibilities. The final three volumes in the Bent series are *Life Histories of North American Cardinals, Grosbeaks, Buntings, Towhees, Finches, Sparrows, and Allies.* They were compiled and edited by Mr. Austin, and published in 1968.

Birds of America, edited by T. Gilbert Pearson with John Burroughs as consulting editor and six assisting editors, Garden City Publishing Company, Inc., Garden City, New York, 1936, 832 pp. and 106 color plates by Louis Agassiz Fuertes. Although this book was first published in 1917, it is an excellent work of reference and is available at bookstores for a price that is modest for such a handsome volume. The text descriptions of birds are very detailed, and the matter about habits and foods is excellent, far exceeding what one finds in a field guide.

Specialized Books

A Guide to Bird Songs, by Aretas A. Saunders, Doubleday & Company, Inc., Garden City, New York, 1951, 307 pp., and diagrams. Descriptions and diagrams according to an ingenious system worked out by the author of the songs and singing habits of 108 land birds of the northeastern states.

Birds of the New York Area, by John Bull, Harper & Row, New York, 1964, 540 pp., with maps and occasional line drawings of birds. This book is indispensable for any birder in the New York area (which in this book includes all of Long Island, parts of Connecticut, and Orange, Putnam, and Westchester counties in New York, and the upper half of New Jersey). The book lists all the birds that have been recorded in the area and how frequently, with early and late dates.

A Laboratory and Field Manual of Ornithology, by Olin Sewall Pettingill, Jr., Burgess Publishing Company, Minneapolis, third edition, 1958, 379 pp., many line drawings. The edition is intended as an aid to ornithological study at the college or university level. It does not pretend to cover the ornithological field, but contains a selection of the more important aspects of ornithology that can be studied during a course in a semester or summer session of the academic year.

The Migrations of Birds, by Jean Dorst, Houghton Mifflin Company, Boston, 1962, 476 pp., and various line sketches. A definitive work by the curator of the Division of Mammals and Birds, the National Museum of Natural History, Paris.

A New Dictionary of Birds, edited by A. Landsborough Thomson, McGraw-Hill Book Company, New York, 1964, 928 pp., 16 plates in color and many others in black and white, often photographs. The title is a tribute to the memory of Alfred Newton, one of the founders of the British Ornithologists' Union, whose *A Dictionary of Birds* (1896) is a classic of ornithological literature. The present work contains definitions of anything you need to know about birds, from *abdomen* to *zygomatic arch* (the bony arch of the cheek).

The Family Life of Birds, photographs and text by Hans D. Dossenbach, McGraw-Hill Book Company, New York, 1971, 192 pp., and many plates and diagrams in color and some black-and-white line sketches. The book is translated from the German. Some of its sections concern migration, the great breeding areas of the world, nest building, and other main phases of birdlife.

There has been a great proliferation of books about birds in the last score of years. I list here only the volumes I use most frequently. There are many excellent regional or local volumes, on *Birds of Washington State,* for instance, or *Birds of North Carolina,* or *Bird Studies at Old Cape May.* There are volumes on particular kinds of birds, such as *Sea-Birds* by James Fisher and R. M. Lockley, or the splendid two-volume edition of *Eagles, Hawks and Falcons of the World,* by Leslie Brown and Dean Amadon, published in 1968 by McGraw-Hill Book Company. There are also books encompassing the birds of the world that the birder may well wish, like E. Thomas Gilliard's *Living Birds of the World,* or Paul Barruel's *Birds of the World.* There can be no formula for the bird watcher's library. He must merely acquire what he needs and what his pocketbook can afford.

10

ENVIRONMENTAL PROTECTION

I confess that I have slight patience with books and lesser documents about environmental protection that merely attempt to arouse the reader to a mild excitement, as enough to induce him to write a letter to his newspaper or congressman. What is required to be of any real significance is personal participation, with daily work and boring chores. I assume that, for the amateur bird watcher, this work is nonpaid. What this chapter is about is the exacting, endless, and frequently tiresome business that is involved in environmental protection, why it is of this nature, and why it is ultimately rewarding.

The logical conclusion of the activity of an amateur birder is to protect the environment in which birds can thrive. How otherwise can his personal program have any useful purpose? There may come a time when he has seen, let us say, 600 species in the United States; or more in his state than anyone else; but eventually the building of lists begins to pall. Why add another species to your New Jersey list if you have seen it already elsewhere in the United States? For that matter, why go to extremes to see an Old World rarity in America when you have seen it already in the Old World, where it was not a rarity?

What of the Amateur?

I mention the amateur bird watcher, because the professional—as one on a museum staff—is obviously in an area where his inquiries can never end. But the amateur, unless he is dedicated to some program of research, as a monograph on the white-throated sparrow, is studying birds for his own pleasure, and the chances are this brings little gain to others. If he cannot help other human beings with his hobby, he might help the birds.

The bird watcher is probably somewhat of a conservationist anyway. The mere fact that he is a member of a bird club means that he is associated with others in the interest of birds. Frank Chapman instituted the Christmas bird counts in 1900, when he was editor of *Bird-Lore,* because he wanted to distract persons' attention from shooting birds to observing, counting, and enjoying them. While the counts are not significant censuses, they do take some 19,000 birders afield every Christmas season, and focus attention on birds as living creatures rather than as inert objects in a game bag.

Growth of Interest

In recent years, since the middle 1960s, there has been an enlarging interest in conservation or, as the term is beginning to be used, environmental protection. Some of this interest can be traced to Rachel Carson's *Silent Spring,* but most of it stemmed from what has become increasingly apparent, that our natural resources are being exhausted or polluted at a rate faster than we can afford if we wish to continue to enjoy clean water, good air, and productive soil.

It is inevitable that a person strives to protect the objects of his affection. At one time I was president of the New Jersey Audubon Society, and the mere exercise of my office meant that I became involved in the acquisition of refuges, the prosecution of hunters who operated pole traps, the institution of state legislation to protect owls and hawks from indiscriminate killing. And the fact that I wrote a weekly newspaper column about birds that was read and enjoyed by close to 100,000 persons increased their appreciation of nature and their own interest in seeing it preserved. In 1968 I was invited to become a trustee of the South Branch Watershed Association in New Jersey. This association is concerned with keeping pure water in the South Branch of the Raritan River that flows into Raritan Bay. We are also concerned with the prevention of erosion, air pollution, and other conservationist causes. Even as a member of the Hunterdon County Bird Club I become active in projects that help the birds.

Beecher Bowdish

An example of how bird watching and conservation go together is Beecher Bowdish, who died in Demarest just before his ninety-first birthday in 1963. Few in the state had done more for conservation, and none was more beloved by bird watchers. He devoted his entire career to the New Jersey Audubon Society. In some of its lean years he seemed to keep it alive almost single-handedly, raising money when the treasury was empty, obtaining new members, leading stirring fights for conservation.

Bowdish signed the society's first annual report in 1911 as its secretary, and when he retired from that post in 1948 he offered a brief summary of the society's course during his stewardship. In 1911 the society had only 200 members; in 1973 it enrolls some 3,600. He said that it took ten years to win state legislation protecting the bobolink as a songbird; the society's first proposed bill was defeated in 1915, enacted in 1921, repealed in 1922, and re-enacted in 1925. Only in the 1960s have hawks and owls been protected from indiscriminate shooting, largely through the efforts of the New Jersey Audubon Society, but back in 1916 Bowdish led successful opposition to a bill that would have put a bounty on all hawks and owls except the osprey.

He inspired the Audubon members to protect nesting cliff swallows in the 1920s, to win enactment in 1935 of legislation designating the goldfinch as the New Jersey state bird, to prohibit commercial gathering of bittersweet, to oppose a shooting season on mourning doves, and in 1935 led the Society in its successful fight against the Passaic Valley Flood Control Commission's proposal to flood Troy Meadows, still the best freshwater marsh along the Atlantic Seaboard and a splendid place to find marsh birds.

Bowdish was also a bird bander. When he stopped banding in 1958, he had pursued this activity for forty-five years. Among other species, he ringed 12,292 sparrows and 4,856 warblers. Among the sparrows, the white-throats were most frequently banded, with 5,761, and the rarest sparrow was the grasshopper, with only one tagged. Most numerous warbler was the myrtle, with 2,024 banded, and rarest were the Lawrence's, Brewster's, prothonotary, and Cape May, with one or two each.

My first contact with Bowdish was in 1926 when I was a newspaper editor and delivered a series of talks on natural history over Radio Station WODA in Paterson, under the sponsorship of the Izaak Walton League. Bowdish heard the talks and invited me to join the New Jersey Audubon Society. I did not accept this invitation for eighteen years, but when I wrote him eventually, asking to be enrolled, he declared it was never too late. He was still a member of the board of directors when I became president a decade later.

What I want to write about here is not the general subject of conservation, but grass-roots conservation as I know it from the point of view of a chairman of an environmental commission in a municipality in New Jersey.

The Environmental Problem

I suppose the general environmental problem could be stated in terms of my conversation one day in 1963 when in Washington I had the opportunity to ask Dr. Richard H. Holton, the U.S. Department of Commerce's Assistant Secretary for Economic Affairs, a question: "What will be the effect on our economic growth of the depletion of our natural resources?" I instanced the pollution of water, the destruction of forests, and the rapid use of our mineral deposits. We did not discuss aesthetic values, because this did not seem his especial province.

His reply, essentially, was that we would be able to find synthetic substitutes or to import the basic materials that we will need.

Since then, there has been a more detailed estimate in a report by a foundation called Resources for the Future and published by Johns Hopkins Press. The gist of this report is an answer to the question of whether the United States can count upon sufficient natural resources to meet its needs over the next thirty years.

In respect to water, the main problem in the East will be how much of the water is fit to use. It will be the problem of enough storage capacity to dilute the concentration of pollution and the more thorough treatment of waste water.

In respect to forests, the demand for forest products by the year 2,000 will be so great that the only answer will be more intensive management of existing forests, intensified efforts to find substitutes, and larger imports.

In respect to land, the demand for recreational space will be such that a "land deficit" of 50 million acres is expected. The only solution suggested is multiple use of land, as in devoting more forest and grazing land to recreational use.

In respect to vanishing supplies of petroleum and natural gas, the solution is nuclear energy, and, in respect to depletion of nonfuel minerals, it is imports or commercial exploitation of now costly or inaccessible deposits. Already in 1973, conservationists are worried about an approaching energy crisis, when because of lack of fuel, there might not be enough energy to light or heat buildings, to provide air conditioning, to operate trains and buses.

One of the major problems of years to come must be the conflict between ecology and economics, or how much will our efforts to keep the country a pleasant place to live retard its economic growth and sufficiency.

Environmental Commissions

The easiest and best way for a bird watcher (or anyone else) to take an active part in the protection of the environment is to work on or with an environmental commission. These commissions exist in seven states, and they should exist in fifty. They are functioning units of municipal government whose purpose is to promote the conservation and development of a municipality's natural resources. They are responsible for providing the impetus and taking the leadership in natural resources planning at a local level where no organized effort toward these ends has been noticeable in the past.

A commission's efforts are devoted to planning, implementing, and informing the public about local conservation programs. It produces natural resources inventories, plans and projects for development, and recommends conservation measures to be included by municipal planning boards in master plans for land use. It can accept gifts of land, interests therein or funds, or apply for grants to acquire land, all on behalf of the municipality's conservation purposes. It can manage land for conservation purposes and operate conservation programs. It can act as the coordinating agency of the community on conservation matters and as liaison between local conservation needs and regional, state, and federal agencies administering to those needs. The top such agency in New Jersey is the State Department of Environmental Protection, and it is a large, powerful, and highly effective organization.

Mission and Membership

Legislation establishing municipal conservation commissions was enacted in New Jersey in May 1968, following the lead of several New England states. For instance, commissions had been in operation in Massachusetts since 1957, and 281 had been set up in only three subsequent years. New Hampshire, Maine, and Connecticut followed. After the enactment of the enabling legislation in New Jersey, the growth in number of commissions was also rapid. When my own commission was established in February 1971, there were 80 such in the state, but exactly two years later there were 200. I attended the annual meeting of the Association of New Jersey Environmental Commissions in Morristown in January 1973 and was amazed to find the attendance around 900. Governor Cahill, who spoke, was also astonished at the number of persons there.

An environmental commission (the name was changed from conservation commission by state legislation in 1972) consists of from five to seven members, all residents of the municipality and one of them also a member of the municipal planning board. It is mainly an advisory group, helping the municipal government. Members are appointed by the mayor and initially have terms of one to three years, staggered, but all subsequent appointments are for three years.

Powers of the commission are several:

1. to conduct research into the use and possible use of open land areas

2. to coordinate activities of unofficial bodies organized for similar purposes

3. to prepare, advertise, print, and distribute books, maps, plans, charts, and pamphlets as it deems necessary for its purposes

4. to prepare and keep an index of open areas, publicly or privately owned, including open marshlands, swamps, and other wetlands

5. to obtain information on the proper use of such areas

6. to recommend to the planning board or governing body plans and programs for inclusion in a master plan, and for development and use of such areas

7. to acquire, subject to the approval of the governing body, property both real and personal, in the name of the municipality, by gift, purchase, or other means

What Value a Commission?

The chief value to a community of an environmental commission is that the municipality acquires a governmental body that is concerned solely with natural resources and their conservation. The activities and interests of the commission are not diluted by the necessity of day-to-day administration, as in the case of the township committee; nor by conflicts between the zoning ordinance and private interest, as in the case of the board of adjustment; nor by subdivision control, as in the case of the planning board. The environmental commission is able to devote its energies toward maintaining the wholesome, pleasing environment which is daily becoming more necessary for a community and more difficult to achieve and preserve. The environmental commission enlists in the service of the community conservation-minded citizens who work without any compensation.

In New Jersey in August 1972, the scope of the environmental commissions was broadened by an amendment to the 1968 act. The amendment provided that the commissions "shall have power to study and make recommendations concerning open space preservation, water resources management, air pollution control, solid waste management, noise control, soil and landscape protection, environmental appearance, marine resources, and protection of flora and fauna." Our commission in Alexandria Township had assumed from the beginning that this generally was our natural province, so the new legislation really made no difference to us. An official organization that is nonpaid and whose guidelines are not specifically established has latitude in the execution of its program. After all, its position is mainly advisory, so what does it or anyone else have to lose if it uses its imagination?

Community's Attitude

It would appear that the purposes of an environmental commission are laudable and desirable from the point of view of the community's welfare, yet this is not necessarily apparent to the populace. Much depends upon the nature of the community. When our commission was created in 1971, I was surprised to find that three of our five commissioners were dubious about the whole thing. At one point I had to ask one of them if he considered "conservation" to be a dirty word. The idea of having a commission was originated by a friend of mine and myself, and the outgoing mayor was induced to approve it. The succeeding mayor appointed the members of the commission, and he may have done the best he could in selecting personnel, because in a rural place such as ours there are few persons who have the ability to serve on such a governmental body and fewer still who have any understanding of ecological problems. Moreover, there are not many persons who care. This is essentially a farming community of 2,600 population (although the complexion of the township is rapidly changing from farmland to suburban), and the farmers seem to be more concerned about their license to use their land as they wish than to be governed by ecological considerations. If they want to build on flood plains, they resent being restricted from doing so. If they want to build on 35-degree slopes, they consider that this is only their own business, with no regard to the effect that runoff may have on soil erosion and effluent disposal. If they want to build houses, they want to build any kind that suits their fancies and pocketbooks, irrespective of any building code.

Cautious Procedure

The result was that our commission had to proceed cautiously, because an environmental group must consider the political situation in a community. Three of our five members were afraid of arousing the apprehension or antagonism of persons or groups in the township. So, we started with simple projects that could hardly arouse the suspicion of anyone. One of our first was to measure the level of water in wells, as our community depends upon private wells and has no municipal water supply and, for that matter, no municipal sewerage system. We got the Township Committee to require the building inspector to distribute to the builders or owners of new houses leaflets we prepared telling how to install well gauges. These, essentially, are plastic tubes that can be inserted in a well, attached to a pump and a gauge, and when air is pumped into the tube the gauge measures the depth of water in the well. The tubes were installed by the well drillers and the reading was done by the South Branch Watershed Association. This was an obviously good move, because many wanted to know the depth of water in their wells, especially in dry years. We had good acceptance of this project from builders of houses and no objection from anyone.

Another project was more complicated. At first we wanted a stream analysis, from chemical, physical, and biological aspects, done by graduate students in ecology at Lehigh University. We got an estimate of $386, but the mayor opposed the project, because he said he knew the streams were polluted by houses and farms and that, if there was a demand to have them cleaned, he would be forced to install a very expensive sewer system. We acceded to this position, because we felt it was better to have the support of the mayor on our overall program than merely to analyze streams.

Analysis of Well Water

Somewhat later, however, we talked with the head of the ecology department at Lehigh University (Dr. E. E. MacNamara, who was killed in an airplane accident in 1973), and arranged another project. This was a study by some of his graduate students of the water in 44 wells and springs in our township. This, of course, was underground water, instead of surface water as suggested in the first project. Our commission made the arrangements with owners of the wells for the students to sample them, and the students analyzed the water for 17 elements, all chemical rather than biological. The conclusion was that the water in the wells was potable from the point of view of state standards, and that it was adequate in supply for a reasonable amount of residential development, although more intensive building might require the drilling of deeper wells.

Flood Plains

These were two simple experiments in conservation, and from these we proceeded to more complex. One ordinance that we drafted and induced our township to enact concerned building on flood plains. The streams in New Jersey, Pennsylvania, and New York are subject to severe flooding, and persons who in former years built their houses too near the water were inundated, as along the Passaic River in New Jersey. Our state recently legislated a flood insurance program, which meant that property owners affected would be eligible for governmentally subsidized flood insurance from insurance companies if the community had enacted a flood-plains ordinance, restricting building on the plains.

It was somewhat puzzling to us, in a pleasing way, that the township adopted this ordinance so readily, and it was one of the first in our county to be enacted. Other municipalities had found that citizens opposed flood-plains ordinances because they did not wish to be restrained in any way in the use of their land. Probably the main reason we had so little difficulty was that the township's residents could not be eligible for this flood insurance unless there was a flood-plains ordinance. Alexandria residents were declared eligible for flood insurance early in 1973.

Soil Conservation District

A municipal environmental commission can gain from co-operation with its county Soil Conservation District. In our Hunterdon County the conservation district is a governmental subdivision of the state of New Jersey and a unit of the Soil Conservation Service, which is a federal service, and a division of the U.S. Department of Agriculture. The district's specific purpose is to administer a program to protect, improve, and utilize the natural resources of the district, including soil, water, air, wildlife, forests, agricultural land, and open space in conformance with the concept of total watershed management. The district cooperates with county planning boards, townships, and other municipalities, environmental commissions, municipal planning boards, as well as citizen organizations and persons interested in wise use of our resources.

Memorandum of Understanding

Our Alexandria environmental commission was helped in its program by a so-called memorandum of understanding between the township and the County Soil Conservation District. This document stipulated various activities by both the district and the municipality, the major premise being that both these bodies have responsibilities for protecting and developing natural resources within their respective boundaries. Specifically, the district agreed to assist in conducting inventories of natural resources, interpret soil surveys, identify land-use limitations, and make recommendations for the use of land. It also agreed to cooperate with the municipal engineer in analyzing drainage, erosion, and sediment problems. The municipality agreed to observe the principles of sound soil and water conservation, giving consideration to the need for adequate drainage facilities, erosion-control measures, stabilization of sediment-producing areas, woodland and wildlife management, proper effluent disposal, and aesthetic improvement.

This agreement helped us to get the municipality to pass our flood-control ordinance, because the question naturally arose as to how the flood plains could be delineated. In some areas of New Jersey these plains have been mapped by the Army Corps of Engineers, but only along the Raritan River basin in Hunterdon County. My township is mainly in the Delaware River basin and its flood plains have not been mapped. However, the Soil Conservation District has what it calls soil maps, which show the kinds of soil in all the municipalities in the county. Soil that has been deposited by water is considered to be in a flood plain and not suitable for buildings. If any doubt developed about a particular site, the district agreed it would inspect the spot and resolve the doubt for us.

Conservation Ordinances

The agreement with the District helped us to formulate a Land Disturbance Ordinance to Control Soil Erosion and Sedimentation. The purpose of the act was to control soil erosion and sediment damages by requiring adequate provisions for surface water retention and drainage and for the protection of exposed soil surfaces. In our ordinance we required that the developer or other applicant to disturb land had to submit to the governing body a plan to provide for soil erosion and sediment control for each site. The plan had to contain location and description of existing natural and man-made features on and surrounding the site, location and description of proposed changes to the site, and measures for soil erosion and sediment control which had to meet or exceed "Standards and Specifications for Soil Erosion and Sediment Control in Urbanizing Areas," promulgated by the Soil Conservation Service. This is a large volume that we placed on file in the office of the township clerk.

Another ordinance we proposed to the Township Committee provided for the regulation of disturbance of soil and the construction of buildings or other structures on critical slope areas. As an example of a bad situation, I recall one day when I was asked to meet with various county and municipal officials to inspect a site where a man wanted to build a house on a slope of 45 degrees, where the effluent could drain down into an attractive brook and soil could be washed into the brook and onto a subtending road. The net effect of the ordinance is that anyone who intends to disturb the soil in any steep-slope situation has to prove that his action will not affect the environment adversely.

Gypsy Moth Control

The relationship between birds and the environment is readily apparent in the problem of gypsy moths. In 1970, the first year in which the moths infested our township, they affected 680 acres, but rather lightly. We expected to suffer more seriously in the years immediately ahead. The moth was first found in New Jersey in 1920, but it was not until 1963 that infestations from neighboring states spread over wide areas, and it became apparent that complete elimination of the pest was not feasible.

Defoliation first appeared in 1966 in Morris County, but only 5 acres were stripped by the leaf-eating caterpillars. In 1972, it was estimated that more than 200,000 acres in the state were affected.

In New Jersey the Department of Agriculture relies more upon biological controls than it does upon spraying with chemicals. It soon began to be realized that the moth was so firmly established in the state that it could only be controlled, not completely destroyed. Biological controls used are largely parasitical flies, wasps, and beetles from overseas countries such as Spain, India, and Yugoslavia. These counterforces are raised in huge numbers in the department's Division of Plant Industry in Trenton, and then released in areas of gypsy moth infestation. Between 1963 and 1970 the division of plant industry raised and released some 80 million parasites. The goal is a population balance between gypsy moths and the predators; the biologist in charge of this program believes that he may have to start releasing gypsy moths here and there to provide a steady food for the parasites.

One such parasite is a fly, *Strumia scutellata.* I took some from the laboratory and released them in our oak grove, although there were no gypsy moths apparent then. The following year, however, I did find some gypsy moth egg masses on the trees. Some had been penetrated probably by wasps (*Ooencyrtus kuwanae*) released by the government. However, we had relatively few egg masses.

Persons tend to become rather panicky when the moths begin to infest their trees, and may demand spraying programs in the hope that the insects can be eliminated completely. DDT is no longer used, but the chemical Sevin (carbaryl) is most often employed. However, Sevin is nonselective, in that it kills beneficial insects, such as honeybees, as well as gypsy moths, and has been linked to birth defects in dogs and rodents.

Homeowners can avoid defoliation and any tree mortality by ground-based spraying of their shade trees with selective, safe, microbial insecticides (Thuricide and Biotrol). Such sprays kill selectively only caterpillars, and do it in the limited trouble spots where these nuisance insects create problems, as in yards or heavily used areas such as picnic grounds.

A promising means of controlling gypsy moths is a bacterial insecticide, the active ingredient of which is *Bacillus thuringiensis,* which has been marketed under the trade name of Biotrol and Thuricide. Sprayed on trees, either from the ground or by the air, this material is ingested by the larvae as they feed. Thereupon their digestive apparatus becomes paralyzed, they cannot eat, and they die. These substances also have an adverse effect upon some other Lepidoptera (butterflies and moths), but unlike Sevin they do not kill the Hymenoptera (bees and wasps). Neither has any harmful effect on human beings or animals. The most heavily infested areas of our township were sprayed with Sevin in 1973.

Jockey Hollow Infestation

A case problem is Jockey Hollow area of Morristown National Historical Park. A few gypsy moth egg masses were found there in 1959, and the National Park Service of the Department of the Interior, which is responsible for the administration of the park, agreed to a one-shot aerial application of DDT in 1960. A few years later a new infestation was noted, and by 1968 a survey found 1,000 acres to be under moderate to heavy attack, with the infestation spreading. Quite suddenly and dramatically in the summer of 1970 the infestation in Jockey Hollow collapsed. As the numbers of the pest insect increased, exceeding carrying capacity of the habitat, a virus, wilt disease, began to take a heavy toll, and vast numbers of parasites and other natural predators finished the job. In 1971 it was practically impossible to find any significant gypsy moth egg masses in Jockey Hollow, and the natural collapse of the pest there has spread to outlying areas.

What damage had the moths inflicted in Jockey Hollow? There were 1,150 forested acres in the park, with 124.3 trees per acre and a total of 142,830 trees. The number of oaks per acres was 27.4, or a total of 31,150, and those that died because of gypsy moth attacks were estimated at 8.8 per acre, or a total of 10,120 dead oaks. Thus, the mortality was 32.11 percent, but there was another 22.63 percent of the oaks in declining health. The number of *all* dead trees in the park attributed to gypsy moths was 10,580.

Green Acres

A broad-based program for acquiring open land is what we in New Jersey have called Green Acres. In 1971 the voters approved legislation that appropriated $80 million for the acquisition of open land for recreational purposes, scenic values, and environmental protection. Municipalities that applied for Green Acres grants could expect only half the cost of the land from the state, but had to provide the other half themselves or perhaps procure it in a matching grant from a federal agency, such as the Bureau of Outdoor Recreation of the Department of the Interior or the Department of Housing and Urban Development.

The Township Committee of Alexandria believed it would be well to apply for land along Nishisakawick Creek, a beautiful stream that flows through Alexandria and Kingwood Townships and Frenchtown to the Delaware River. This stream runs through a rather rugged area that is subtended by a rough road along which some intrepid souls have built houses. It is called The Creek Road. The creek has on some of its northern edge a steep cliff of some 100 feet in height, but on the southern side there is generally a small flood plain upon whicn the township forbids building. The cliff is rich with ferns and other vegetation, and the flood plain is ideal for picnicking, walking, or fishing.

These applications are complex, as there are two, one to the Green Acres assistance program, and the other to the federal agency that hopefully might provide half the funds. Necessary maps delineating the perimeters of the property desired, its acreage, appraisals of its value, title searches for the past five years, and surveys are all needed in duplicate or triplicate. The property we want is 43 acres, worth $69,000 at assessed valuation, in nine parcels owned by seven property owners. At this writing the Bureau of Outdoor Recreation says it has obligated its half of the money, so there is a very good chance we will get a matching grant from the state Green Acres. However, soon thereafter, both federal and state funds were depleted.

Birders and Environmentalists

I suggested earlier in this discussion that the logical end of a bird watcher's career should be to become active in the protection of the environment for birds. The development of environmental commissions, in my own state at least, during the past few years, demonstrates that this is excitingly true. In early 1973 I attended the annual meeting of the New Jersey Association of Environmental Commissions, and, among the persons who were there, I saw many whom I had known only as bird watchers. There was Norman Brydon, for instance, who edited the newsletter of the Association, is a member of the environmental commission in Caldwell, and used to be president of the New Jersey Audubon Society when there were no commissions. There was John Neal, who was formerly president of New Jersey Audubon Society and head of the Morris Nature Club when there were no commissions, and now he is a member of the Morristown Environmental Commission. Morton Cooper is a leading birder in the Toms River area, and I knew him as such before he became chairman of the environmental commission in that area. I could go on and instance many dozens of persons I knew as birders who are now environmental commissioners without, however, abandoning their interest in birds. This, I suppose, is my theme, because it has been my own experience.

Gamwing

I am not sure that Indians should be included in a chapter on conservation, yet the values they cherished are quite parallel with those of our present ecology. Priscilla and I are members of South Branch Watershed Association, with headquarters in nearby Clinton, and the Association determined to hold in the fall of 1970 a Gamwing, which is a kind of Indian harvest festival. This went on for three days, and was a most exhausting operation for us because of the work involved. Idea was to raise money, 40 percent of which would go to the Indians. The net effect of this experiment, to which some 6,000 persons were attracted, was that the Indians were delighted with their share and the chance to sell products of their own manufacture, and wanted another Gamwing the following year. All those who had conducted it for the South Branch Watershed Association had depleted their energy and time, however, and were not inclined to repeat the experience.

We had some 200 Indians at the Gamwing, which is a kind of variation of a powwow. Priscilla managed a book stall, with a large display of books about Indians, and there were displays of Indian life and artifacts, as well as many speakers. Most of our Indian guests were Onondagas from New York, but there were also Cherokees Seminoles, and a single Narragansett. Site was Spruce Run Reservoir, a beautiful wildlife area which the guests treated with respect.

From a naturalist's point of view, it was a rewarding experience because of the insight it afforded into the Indians' attitude toward nature and their use, both historical and contemporary, of plants and other natural objects.

Irving Powless, Jr., chief of the Onondagas, discussed the Indians' attitude toward nature. He said his people respected all living things as part of the Great Spirit, and hence never killed more than they needed. He is a hunter, he said, but never shoots more animal food than is necessary to feed his family of five.

Others of the nine persons on the speakers' program also mentioned this trait. I introduced all.

The Indians' quest for food was based upon hunting, fishing, and gathering wild crops. They practiced some agriculture, as did the Woodland Indians in New Jersey, but it was mainly of the three staples, corn, beans, and squash.

The white-tailed deer was of most value to the Indians of the East. It was the best source of meat and of materials that had a wide utility. From the skins the Indians made clothing, moccasins, and thongs. Skins could be tanned in such a way as to make them soft after wetting. The stiff hair from the tail was used for ornaments and embroidery; the antlers provided tool handles and arrow points; hooves supplied glue; sinews were used for thread, bowstrings, and snares; the bones provided bodkins, skin-dressing tools, handles, and ornaments.

All through the summer and fall the women and children gathered wild fruit, berries, and nuts. These included cranberries, gooseberries, blueberries, black and red raspberries, grapes, cherries, and chokeberries. Nuts included acorns from the pin and white oaks, hickory nuts, hazelnuts, beechnuts. In addition to their three staples, the vegetables included wild potatoes (the Irish potato originated in America), wild onions, milkweed, and the root of the water lily. Most Indian groups ate only two meals a day; later, when they came into contact with the whites, they began to eat three.

The Indians also made maple sugar, letting the sap drip into birch buckets. It was used at feasts and ceremonies and on fruits, vegetables, and even fish. When the first sugar of the year was cooked, a small amount was offered to the Great Spirit. This ceremony, the offering of the first fruits or game, was observed with the first preparation of each seasonal food.

Throughout all the rites, ceremonies, and religious observances of the Woodland Indians, tobacco was the thread of communication between the human elements and the spiritual powers.

In the area of medicine, flagroot was carried on the person to keep away snakes; snakeroot was used as a charm for safety on a journey; the root of a species of milkwort was carried for general health; and dogbane was used as a charm against evil influence.

As this book ends, I suppose we should glance back to the beginning. In the foreword, I mentioned some of the potential pleasures of bird watching, and in the ensuing pages have tried to tell how I have realized them. The greatest of these rewards has been the companionship of my wife in pursuing over the years a mutual and delightful interest. We nearly always make trips together, and do so frequently, even if some are not more extensive than walks around our farm. We have found it rewarding to be able to take these mini-walks merely by stepping outside our house, rather than by driving to a distant place. This sympathetic relationship between us is largely a gift of God, resulting only in part from the early recognition of the values we both held and the firm hope that these values would be sustained over the years.

From another point of view, I am happy that what I have learned about birds could be shared with others through my newspaper columns, books, and lectures. The process has kept me in personal contact with hundreds of persons, and these relationships have sometimes ripened into enduring friendships.

A third major gain has been pleasure from learning more about the birds and their engaging characteristics. Even on our 25-acre farm we have found 148 species, and the potential is possibly 168. We are excited by the great horned and screech owls we hear at night and by the unusual species that appear occasionally, such as the goshawk, Lawrence's warbler, and yellow-breasted chat. We have extended our knowledge of birds by trips throughout the United States and to several lands overseas.

But birds are not the only form of wildlife, and we have learned much about flowers and trees, insects, and mammals. The opportunity for inquiry in these areas is, of course, inexhaustible.

Finally, now that I am retired from my daily chores in New York, I have had time to devote to environmental protection. As chairman of our township commission, I have helped to protect the land from floods and to make available to our citizens federally subsidized flood insurance, to control building on steep slopes, to regulate building that might result in soil erosion and sedimentation, to control gypsy moths, and to study the quality of water in our wells. These projects help to protect the environment not only for our citizens but also for our wildlife. Several other projects are now under way, for environmental protection is a never-ending business.

ABOUT THE AUTHOR

Roger Barton's avocation is birds, an interest he has enjoyed since he was a boy growing up in Brooklyn. He used to go before school to Prospect Park to watch them, and, in the subsequent half-century he has lived in New Jersey, he has pursued this hobby actively. He has been president of the New Jersey Audubon Society, and since 1947 has written a weekly column on birds for the editorial pages of the *Newark Sunday News* and, lately, for the *Courier-News*.

His career has been largely in advertising, where he has edited three magazines, produced four books, and lectured at the Columbia University Graduate School of Business. He is a retired lieutenant colonel in the Army of the United States.

Upon his retirement from business in New York, Mr. Barton built a house on 25 acres, largely forested with evergreens, in rural New Jersey, not far from the Delaware River. The farm has attracted 148 species of birds in the seven years he has lived there. He has enlarged his avian interests by travel in most of the United States, including Alaska, and in several lands overseas. He is interested in plants and insects, as well as in birds, but spends much of his time now as chairman of his community's environmental commission, which entails constant attention to the protection of water, soil, and air against disturbance and pollution.